80/20 Landlording

Increase Your 80 & Decrease Your 20!

Sheamus P. Clarke

Scott Stellhorn

Published by: (Night Hawk Systems, LLC)

Book Team

Author and Contributor	Sheamus P. Clarke
Author and Contributor	Scott Stellhorn
Editor/Polisher	Nick Hayden
Cover Design & Artwork	Ryan Hoover Sr.

First Printing

ISBN: 978-0-9960358-0-4

Published by (Night Hawk Systems, LLC)

Acknowledgement

To our wives and families, who allowed us the time to put this book together at the expense of quality time with them.

To all those tenants and applicants who have given us both the wisdom and patience to continue our pursuits with rental properties as Independent Rental Owners.

Introduction

It usually takes a significant emotional event or epiphany to enable someone to make a permanent change. The authors of this book experienced such events that launched them into the world of Real Estate Investing.

Sheamus was working for a privately held company when the executive team underwent significant changes that Sheamus was not happy with and did not want to be a part of. Sheamus looked at what he could do to best secure his and his family's future. He decided to change his employment as well as invest in a rental property.

His new job in software development allowed him to work from home, doing training and support for a small software company. He spent nights and weekends setting up a rental company, reading up on real estate investing and looking at available properties.

He and his wife purchased a fourplex that had been vacant for some time. Over the next few years, they acquired more properties and now manage and maintain 25 properties.

Scott's in-laws were landlords in the 1980s and introduced him to the concept of rental income. His father-in-law did 95% of the repairs on the units, from plumbing to electrical to roofing. Scott gained his training in maintenance from him, which saved him tremendous money in the future.

While in college, Scott purchased his first fixer-upper to rent and sold it the first year to the tenants who occupied the home.

He graduated college in 1983 with an Associate's Degree in computer science and started his computer technology career writing COBOL for a distribution company in Fort Wayne.

While working full-time, he increased his holdings on fixer-upper multi-unit buildings and, in turn, increased his rental income. As you will read in the upcoming chapters, there were times of joy mixed with "What am I doing?" In the end, the benefits of being an Independent Rental Owner outweighed the issues he encountered.

Forward

Between the two of us, there is more than 45 years of combined landlord experience. From this comes endless lessons and stories.

What you will find in this book is a compilation of the trials and tribulations we have experienced—the extraordinary work required in evictions, small claims, maintenance, property management, and people skills.

You might think this book is simply about terrible tenant experiences. Believe us, we could have written that book. But, for every really bad tenant we've had, we've had even more great tenants. Some tenants have become friends. We've invited them to our homes, celebrated birthdays and holidays with them. We've decided to share a few stories about those tenants as well.

There is also a lot of work that has nothing to do with the properties themselves, issues arising from laws, regulations, and local ordinances. So we decided to give examples of how the eviction and small claims processes work, also.

But why call this book 80/20 Landlording?

It's rooted in something known as the Pareto principle, which states that in many cases, roughly 80% of the effects comes from 20% of the causes.

Business-management consultant Joseph M. Juran suggested the principle and named it after Italian economist Vilfredo Pareto, who observed in 1906 that 80% of the land in Italy was owned by 20% of the population; Pareto also observed that 20% of the pea pods in his garden contained 80% of the peas.

It's become a common rule of thumb in business. For example, someone might say, "Eighty percent of your sales come from 20% of your clients."

It's not hard to find other applications for entrepreneurs and business managers:

- Eighty percent of a company's profits come from 20% of its customers.
- Eighty percent of a company's complaints come from 20% of its customers.
- Eighty percent of a company's profits come from 20% of the time its staff spend.
- Eighty percent of a company's sales come from 20% of its products.
- Eighty percent of a company's sales are made by 20% of its sales staff.

Knowing this, many businesses can improve profitability by focusing on the most effective areas and by eliminating, ignoring, automating, delegating, or retraining the rest, as appropriate.

These ideas are transferable to the Independent Rental Owner.

For instance, it's useful to remember that during a normal day, only 20% of your activity really matters—the most important 20% of your effort produces 80% of your results. Identify and focus on those things in your 20%. Remind yourself of this vital 20% when the fire drills of everyday life happen. If something in the schedule has to slip, if something isn't going to get done, make sure it's not part of that 20%.

Another truth from the landlord business is this: Twenty percent of your tenants will cause 80% of your headaches.

This book is written so that you can focus more on the 20% of your work that matters and less on the 20% of your tenants that cause all the headaches.

We've learned a lot over our 45 combined years. We've found tricks and tools that work. We'll refer to one again and again—Real Tenant History (www.realtenanthistory.com). But there are plenty of others, from legal processes to hard-won knowledge. It's all here to aid you whatever might come.

Being a landlord is not easy, but it *is* rewarding. We hope our experiences, written by landlords, for landlords, can make your work that much easier and that much more rewarding.

Real Tenant History

In this book you will see references to Real Tenant History (https://Realtenanthistory.com).

Real Tenant History is an Internet Based Software Product. We specialize is providing landlord and property managers with the best possible tools for managing their rental units. This Website will be launching in the second quarter of 2014. Feel free to visit the site and signup for our newsletter as a way to keep informed about the launch date.

Sheamus P. Clarke

Scott Stellhorn

1 - The Half-Naked Tenant

One of the many lessons I learned as a landlord is to never enter a renter's apartment alone, and I learned this lesson on a particularly, shall we say, *memorable* visit with a tenant.

Susan's rent was late, so I stopped by to remedy the situation. The lights were on, so I figured someone was home. I rang the doorbell.

No answer.

There's a reason I have keys to all my apartments. I unlocked the door and stepped in, yelling for the tenant.

No answer.

She wasn't going to avoid me so easily. I proceeded up the stairs to the landing, yelled again.

No answer.

I was this far in, why not go all the way? I climbed the rest of the stairs to the foyer and announced myself one last time.

She walked in out of the kitchen. Good news: She was home. Bad news: She was wearing a cut-off T-shirt. And nothing else.

I headed back down the stairs a bit. "Put some clothes on!" I told her.

She ignored me and came to the front door anyway. I stayed where I was, determined to finish what I had started.

"Your rent's late."

"I'm moving in two weeks."

"Your rent's still late."

"I'm not going to pay any more rent. I'm moving. I'm done with paying rent."

Well. It's that easy, is it?

But this is when I decided I would never enter an apartment alone. If I pressed the subject now, the discussion could get ugly, fast, and in her current...state...who knew what she would claim happened afterward. I didn't want to find out.

So I retraced my steps and headed to the local police station.

"Do you have an officer available? I need to speak to a tenant of mine and I have a feeling there might be issues."

It was as simple as asking.

I returned to the apartment, officer now at my side, and knocked. Susan took her time coming to the door. At least she was fully dressed this time.

I explained the situation clearly: "You need to pay your back rent, or you'll be forced to leave the apartment immediately."

She looked at the officer. "He can't do that, can he? He can't kick me out on the spot."

"No, he can't," said the officer.

She gave me a smug grin and told me to "kiss her ass."

"Officer," I said, "I've noticed that the front and back doors are in need of repair. I think I'll remove them tonight. If she's staying, I should get them fixed."

"You can't do that," Susan said. "He can't do that, either, right, Officer?"

He thought a moment. "Well, they are his doors."

So I popped the hinges off the front and back doors and placed them in my truck.

Later that evening, the phone rang. It was Susan's ex-boyfriend, the father of her children. He told me I had to replace the doors immediately. "My kids live over there. Put the doors back on. I'll hold you responsible if anything happens to them."

"Go over and pick them up if you're worried. The doors are in need of repair."

"I can't pick them up. Susan has a restraining order against me."

Ah. Go figure.

"Well, I'm sorry, but this is an issue between me and my tenant. I cannot discuss it with you any further. Good-bye."

She ended up moving the next weekend.

Of course, I still didn't have my rent, so I took her to small claims court. I filled out the proper paperwork, sent it to my attorney. He filed it and three months later appeared in court on my behalf.

Susan contested the claim and was pissed because I wasn't there in person. She believed I had wasted her time.

The second hearing was four weeks later. She decided to not show up so that she could waste *my* time. Lucky me. I received default judgment in the case.

And I happened to know where she worked, so my attorney filed for a payroll garnishment. I got $50 weekly out of her.

But the story didn't end there.

About six months later, I received a phone call from the Department of Family Services for the county her apartment was in. They had some questions about a welfare form I had filled out on Susan's behalf.

"I don't remember ever filling out a form for her," I told them.

After that, I went to the courthouse to get a copy of the supposed form. My suspicions were correct. My signature had been forged.

I submitted the form and four copies of my signature to the local police department, and charges were filed against my tenant.

ARRESTS

A year later, I received a call from the prosecuting attorney for the county asking for more information about the case. Apparently, Susan had not only forged my signature, but also forged a signature on a Medicaid form.

In the end, Susan received nine months of house arrest for her crimes.

And I did get all my back rent. It just took two-and-a-half years.

Here's the takeaway: One can never be too careful when confronting a tenant. It's always better to have a second pair of eyes to witness any discussion. Especially if that discussion involved a half-naked lady.

2 - How to Empty a Property
(The Wrong Way)

It was the Spring of 1995. There, on a certain street, was a fourplex, in desperate need of repair. Next to it were two duplexes, in the same incredible state of disrepair.

And so in the Spring of 1995, I purchased them.

I decided to remodel the duplexes first. I did all the work myself—new siding, new roofs, new drywall, new carpet, new cupboards, new bathrooms, new heating and cooling, new windows, new doors...new everything.

It took a year.

During this time, I informed the tenants of the fourplex that I would soon turn to remodeling their units. Finally, in April 1996, I sent letters stating I'd start work on the fourplex in June. Their leases would not be renewed.

The two-bedroom units were downstairs and the one-bedroom units upstairs. All the apartments had front entrances.

One of the main remodeling tasks was moving the upstairs entrances to the back, adding a huge deck, and adding a carport. This would reduce the traffic in front of the fourplex, give the tenants personalized parking, and allow them to enter from the rear.

These changes required some demolition work that necessitated all the apartments to be empty. The upstairs tenants moved out in May.

The downstairs tenants remained at the beginning of June.

Now, I was new to the rental business. I had about two years under my belt. I wasn't up to speed on all the laws, rules, and ordinances yet.

So when June arrived, I visited the two remaining tenants. They informed me they did not want to move.

"I'm living paycheck to paycheck," said the first tenant. "I don't have the funds for a deposit at a new place right now."

He had been a good tenant, always current on his rent. "Tell you what," I said, "I'll let you sign a lease for a two-bedroom apartment a few blocks over and I won't charge the deposit. The apartment is in better condition than this one, so the rent's a bit more, and you're responsible for all utilities except trash removal, but that's what I have to offer."

He agreed and moved the next weekend.

One tenant down, one to go.

The final tenant was an older woman who had her two sons living with her, aged 24 and 26. She had been a tenant when I purchased the property, so I never made a big deal about how many adults were living in the unit.

Her rent was usually a week late, she never paid her late fees, her front and back porches were always littered with trash, and whenever I visited, I smelled the distinct aroma of marijuana.

Here's our drug policy:

ILLEGAL DRUGS. *If at any time during the lease period illegal drugs are found or heard to be on premises, tenant forfeits all rights to property and will vacate the premises immediately. This does not relieve tenant of obligations described earlier in the lease.*

Though I knew the tenant and her sons were smoking marijuana in my unit, I never did anything about it because I knew I was going to empty the property for remodeling.

It was now the middle of June. I was ready to start the demolition. I had all my permits. The utilities were already in my name, since the tenants did not pay utilities. But after many conversations, the tenant still would not vacate the premises.

I decided to persuade her the easiest way I knew how.

I started upstairs. I removed all the windows and doors. I proceeded to the empty downstairs apartment and did the same. Next, I came to her apartment. I could not enter the apartment and start removing windows, so I removed the front and back doors and cut out all the door jams instead.

That day I also had all the utilities shut off--gas, water, sewer, and electric.

I received a phone call that afternoon. Apparently, she didn't have any power.

"I've turned off all the utilities for the remodeling, " I told her. "They should be back on in about four months."

She called me many, many names and promised she would contact the police. But when she called, they told her this was a civil matter, not a criminal one, and so they couldn't do anything about it.

She lasted through the end of the week. By Sunday, the apartment was empty.

And, yes, they put lots of effort into trashing the place. They overturned the stove and fridge. They yanked cupboards off the wall. They shattered the windows.

It didn't matter. I was in the middle of a demolition, after all.

And now that the property was empty, I turned the utilities back on so I could proceed.

When I cleared out the apartment, I found some interesting things.

I removed some of the untouched cupboards from the kitchen and found their stash of marijuana—a few joints and a couple baggies.

Also, beneath the carpet were three *more* layers of carpet. I guess when one carpet got dirty, they just put down another. Between two layers I found lots of squished dog poo.

The dark spots are dog poop.

Finally, in one of the bedroom heating vents, I found a stash of inappropriate pictures. Perhaps someone had forgotten the hiding place and so left them behind when he moved.

It's amazing what you can find when someone moves out.

I did learn one important lesson in all this—I should have followed the eviction process described later in this book (Chapter 20). If I would have started the process when I first mailed the warning letters in April, I could have saved lots of time and headaches along the way.

Plus, it would have been the *right* way to empty a property.

3 - Things That Go Bump in the Kitchen

Most complaints from a tenant are pretty ordinary. "The sink's leaking." "The lawn needs mowed." "The neighbor's weird-looking." You know, that kind of thing.

Every once in a while, though, an issue comes along that raises your eyebrows and spontaneously elicits a dumbfounded, "Really?"

Here's one of those occasions.

I was renting an apartment to three single girls. They all seemed nice, they all had jobs, and they generally seemed down-to-earth. At least, that was my impression for the first few months.

Then one month they sent a note in with their rent. "We have ghosts in the apartment. Please come by to see what you can do about them."

Well, this perked my interest. I had owned this rental for 15 years and never heard anything like this before. I headed over that night.

All three girls were home, huddled together and on edge. They showed me where they had "seen" the ghosts.

"At night," they said excitedly, "we hear them in the kitchen. Seriously. We all heard them. They bang around and stuff."

I could tell the three were legitimately frightened by what they perceived to be paranormal activity occurring in what I had always assumed was a normal kitchen.

"Can you make them go away?"

They looked at me wide-eyed and pale. What had happened to my three down-to-earth tenants?

"Please?"

How, exactly, was I supposed to make these ghosts "go away"?

I'm a practical guy. I don't believe in ghosts, and I don't really understand why other people do, so I decided to explore the issue. (Why? Because I'm practical.)

One thing I found is that *phasmophobia*, or the fear of ghosts, is difficult to diagnose. While most people experience a certain thrill of anxiety during ghost stories or scary movies, some people cannot deal with the fear it causes. This overwhelming fear is often related to the fear of death.

Did my tenants really believe these kitchen poltergeists wanted to harm them?

To further muddy the issue, obsession with the paranormal can sometimes indicate *magical thinking*, a mental disorder that fixates on irrational correlations between events. Like black cats being bad omens.

But paranormal activities are also studied by some scientists (parapsychology), and in a broader sense are the realm of nearly every faith. To simply discount the presence of ghosts because I didn't believe in them wasn't fair to these girls, who obviously *did* believe in them.

Even though, when they first claimed to have a haunted apartment, I mentally went, "Really?"

What I did find in my studies is that good mental health professionals accept the client's belief in the supernatural regardless of their own personal beliefs.

All right, fine. Spirits are making soufflé in the kitchen.

But while I discovered various coping skills that can be taught to deal with the phasmophobia, and a number of ways to counsel a person affected by it, I'm a landlord, not a therapist. I couldn't prove the ghosts didn't exist and I couldn't, in good conscience, tell these obviously terrified girls to just suck it up and deal with it.

It wasn't worth the effort to work through the fears they had. I didn't want to get calls every week about ghosts. I'm not Bill Murray.

So I decided to let them out of their lease.

There's good news and bad news at the end of this strange little story. The good news is, since it was a nice three-bedroom apartment, I had no trouble renting it almost immediately after the girls left.

The bad news is, I never did determine if there were ghosts in the kitchen.

4 - Applicant Red Flags

You start with an empty apartment.

You put a "For Rent" sign in the yard. It's cheap, it's simple, and it works.

Unless the unit is tucked away in a corner. Then you advertise in the local paper or, to keep up with the times, on the web.

I don't recommend a man dressed in a Statue of Liberty costume, but, hey, it works for tax preparation companies. I guess.

However you get the word out, eventually you'll get a call from a prospective tenant.

I have a list of 15 questions for the initial phone call with a prospective tenant. Depending on how the tenant answers the questions, I may decide not to move to the next step, scheduling a time to show the unit in question.

While using these preliminary questions, I've also learned to recognize a handful of red flags. Here are a few of them.

The "Don't Show Me No Respect" Flag

Ring!

I answer. "Hello?"

"I seen you had a for rent sign, ain't cha?"

Red Flag.

Don't get me wrong. I'm not picky about how people speak. *But* I do expect an attempt at proper etiquette when receiving the initial call about the apartment. If a tenant can't put his best foot forward at the start, what will happen later on?

I want the conversation to go something like this:

Ring!

I answer. "Hello?"

"Hello. This is John Doe, and I saw that you have an apartment for rent."

Pretty simple, I think.

I suppose it's a sign of the current educational system that someone can graduate high school and not know how to properly conjugate a verb.

I'm not a wordsmith, but I can carry on a conversation using the correct words, and I want to expect the same of my tenants.

The "I Need It Now" Flag

Ring!

I answer. "Hello?"

"How much is the rent?"

Oh, I love these calls. Many times, the person doesn't even know how large the apartment is. They need a place *now*, and it doesn't matter how big it is.

When this happens, you have to ask yourself: "Why does this person need an apartment *right now*."

The answer, unfortunately, is often 1.) he's being evicted or 2.) he's leaving his old place in a hurry. Why? Perhaps he has past rent due or he's violated his lease or he's had his utilities turned off.

In most cases, you do not want to rent to someone like this. He's called a "Tenant Predator," and he is trouble.

"The System Is Broken" Flag

Ring!

I answer. "Hello?"

"Hello. My name is Jane Doe, and I saw that you have an apartment for rent. I'm looking for a two-bedroom apartment."

"At the moment, I only have a three-bedroom available."

"That's great! I'm expecting my third child. Another bedroom will come in handy."

"Who else will be living with you?"

"Just me, my boyfriend, and my two children." Then, without prompting, she gives me her current income, breaking it down for me. It's quite the extensive list:

- Social Security Disability for her and her two children
- CANI – Government Assistance
- Aid to Families with Dependent Children
- Utility Assistance from the county for gas, electric, and water
- Food Stamps
- Medicaid Insurance

"I'm in a two-bedroom," she explains, "but if I move into a bigger apartment, my assistance will go up. My utility assistance will go up, too. And once my baby's born, I'll collect SSD for her as well."

"So, what's the total for your assistance and income currently?"

"I get about $3000 a month in assistance, but that'll go up $700 with the baby, and with a three-bedroom, that's another $600 a month."

By now, I'm starting to have trouble keeping track of all the "income" she's receiving, though she obviously has a firm grasp of it. "So, really," she says, "I'll be getting $4300 a month instead of $3000."

If you do the math, she's currently getting $36,000 a year. With a third child and larger apartment, it would rise to $51,000 a year.

Not a bad income. Except it's earned off hard-working taxpayers instead of from her own two hands.

At this point, I ask a question I cannot ask, but I want to be certain the apartment will meet her needs, since she's on Social Security Disability.

"Could you share with me why you're on disability?"

She hesitates. "I was diagnosed as mentally retarded. That was about six years ago, when I dropped out of high school. Since then, I haven't felt I could work, so I've been on disability."

That solidifies my decision.

"Then I'm afraid I cannot rent you the apartment."

"What? Why?"

"You're taking advantage of the system and doing it well. I think that's a pretty good indication how you'll take advantage of me."

End of conversation.

The "What Kind of Dog Exactly?" Flag

Ring.

I answer. "Hello?" We get through the basics. Then, my favorite question from prospective tenants:

"Do you accept pets?"

We accept cats and small dogs who weigh less than 45 pounds at adult weight. Also, we do not accept pitbulls or rottweilers.

Typically, when the pet question comes up, I ask, "What type of pet do you have?"

If they say, "A dog," I dig deeper.

"What type of dog?"

Now, if the response is blue-nose terrier or red-nose terrier or pit dog or bull terrier or bull pit terrier or pit terrier or pit bull terrier or bulldog or Staffordshire Terrier or American bull terrier or Yankee terrier or St. Francis terriers, it all really means one thing--it's a pitbull.

And if they've tried to fudge the answer, I ask, "Why didn't you just say pitbull?"

I've heard some amazing answers to this. My favorite is "Because if I told you it was a pitbull, you wouldn't rent to me."

"Yes, you're right. But that is not why I won't rent to you now."

"Why then? Why won't you rent to me?"

"You tried to lie to me," I say. "And I don't rent to liars."

Conclusion

You can learn a lot from the initial conversation with a prospective tenant. Be observant. Listen carefully. If this isn't the one to rent to, don't worry. The "For Rent" sign is still sitting in the lawn.

5 - They Grow Up So Fast!

Mike and Mary Smith contacted me about a five-bedroom house I had placed an ad for. It was a perfect location for them. They had three children (11, 14, and 19) living with them, as well as Mike's mother, and all the adults worked within five blocks of the house. On nice days, they could all walk to work within 10 minutes.

I thought to myself, "These could be great tenants. They all work and they'll be close to their jobs. Rent shouldn't be a problem."

While Mary filled out the application, Mike shared some of his hopes with me. "I want to get the kids in a better school district, get them a better place to live. This house will be great."

He was articulate, pleasant, and presented himself well.

I did not meet the children at the initial meeting, but most tenants don't bring children to this stage of the process.

At this time I didn't have access to the Real Tenant History tools, but I did my usual checks.

I used the application to verify their employment and called their three personal references. I also performed a sex offender check on all three adults and a background check on Mike and Mary. Only my calls to their prior landlord went unreturned.

Employment checked out. References were glowing. The background check turned up nothing unusual. Everything was perfect.

It never occurred to me to get the children's names and check on them. After all, they were children.

As with most tenants, the first few months were great. Rent was paid on time. Utilities were put into their name and paid. They called when something needed repaired or the grass needed mowed. Everything was still perfect.

Then one month the 10th rolled around and rent, due on the 1st, was still unpaid. I called. I started getting the usual excuses.

Don't get me wrong, they were still great tenants. They paid their rent by the 15th, and they paid the late fees as well. But everything wasn't perfect anymore.

Since Mike, Mary, and Mike's mom worked full-time, they were not typically home during the day. The 11 and 14 year old were in school. This left the 19 year old home. And I started getting calls from the neighbors about his day visitors when he was alone at the house.

I called Mike. That's when I found out what I should have known when the application was filled out. The 19 year old was under house arrest. He couldn't work or leave the house. He had an ankle bracelet provided by the local police.

"That shouldn't be a problem," I told Mike, though he should have told me about his son's predicament, "but your son needs to be careful who he allows on the property."

This was prophetic.

There was a vacant house next door to Mike and Mary's house. I had never met the owner; it had been empty for more than a year.

One particular week, I learned the vacant house had been broken into. Someone had broken the back door and a couple windows. Also, a house two doors down from my rental had been broken into while its owner was away.

Soon I discovered that the son's friends were responsible.

It's part of my responsibility to ensure my tenants and the unit's neighbors have a safe living environment. These friends had made it unsafe. The next time rent was late, I decided to serve an eviction notice.

The family was gone by month's end.

Next came the inspection. I was surprised to find the house was a mess. The family had taken any belongings they needed but had left everything else for me to clean up.

And the stove and refrigerator were gone.

This pissed me off. I called the police to report a theft.

The police took down my statement, and since I had move-in pictures showing the appliances, they had a detailed description of what had been taken. But since I had not seen the tenants take the appliances, it would be hard to prove, legally, that they were the ones who stole them.

After two days of general cleaning and two more of repairs, I was calm enough to call Mike and discuss the stolen appliances.

Here's what Mike told me: "I thought since the stove and fridge were in the property when we rented it, they were ours, so we took them when we left."

"If you look at the lease," I said, incredulous, "you'll see that we provided those appliances while you lived here, but they belong to me."

"I've lost my copy of the lease, but I think you're wrong." And he hung up.

Two days later, Mary called. "I talked to Mike about the conversation you had with him, but we didn't take the stove or the fridge. When we left, they were still in the house."

Of course.

Now it was my word against theirs. Since they were all employed, I decided to take them to small claims court. I hoped to recoup past rent, cleaning and repairing fees, and the cost of a stove and refrigerator.

Everyone showed up at the hearing, and I did recoup the rent and cleaning fees, but I was out of luck on the appliances. It was just my word against theirs.

So here's the moral of the story: When you rent to a family, make sure you know all the "adults" who will be living in the unit, not just the parents.

This was a good example of a tenant telling me everything he wanted me to know and "forgetting" to tell me important details that might weigh against him.

Finally, one last bit of advice: Having move-in and move-out pictures documented and saved is immensely helpful. With today's technology, all you need is a smartphone to snap the pictures. And with Real Tenant History, you can store these pictures with the lease and print them for reference whenever you need to.

6 - Another Death in the Family

A few years ago I had a tenant who always, without fail, paid her rent late.

Every month, on the first of the month, I would receive a letter explaining why the rent would be late.

Now, I appreciated the heads-up and normally I waived the late fee since she notified me ahead of time. She was an older lady, and I didn't feel right charging her the fee. And, most times, she paid within 10 days.

We had a nice rhythm going.

I always filed away her monthly letters. I wanted to keep a record of our communication, just in case.

One month, the letter stated her mother had passed away and she had to travel to make the funeral arrangements. Her mother lived in the southern half of the state, so my tenant had to make multiple trips in preparing the funeral.

The letter was two-pages, handwritten. She went into great detail about the costs associated with the funeral, travel, lodging, and so on.

It tickled something in the back of my brain.

I pulled out my file of letters and I found what my unconscious had been looking for. The previous year, she had also written that her rent would be late because her mother died.

It seems rumors of her mother's death had been widely exaggerated.

I decided to stop by her apartment. Just to make sure I hadn't misunderstood something, I took copies of her letters.

I knocked.

"Who's there?"

"Your landlord."

This particular tenant always came to the door in a bathrobe, and this was no exception. I don't know why. I never went in the apartment alone because of this, and I think she knew I wouldn't.

"What do you want?" she asked.

"I'm sorry to hear that your mother passed away. If there's anything I can do to help, just let me know."

"Thank you. That's very kind."

"I'm confused about one thing, though. I was looking through my records and it seems you sent a similar letter last year."

"I—I don't know what you mean."

I pulled out both letters. "I think if you look at them, it'll jog your memory. Maybe you can explain it to me."

She took the letters and began to read.

Then, suddenly, she shut the door in my face.

Later that day, I tried calling her, but no one answered. The next day, I tried the phone again. Still no one.

I did receive a phone call from the tenant above her. "It looks like she's moving out," he told me. It wouldn't be the first time one of my tenants moved without notice.

Sunday, I went over to check out the situation myself. Sure enough, she was gone.

Her mother's two deaths must really have affected her.

Now, the lease is specific about notices and late fees. In order to *not* have the lease automatically renewed for the next month, either the tenant or the landlord must give a 30-day written notice.

It was nearly mid-June. She owed for June and, without a written notice, for July as well.

That didn't include the late fees, which are pretty simple: $75 if rent is not postmarked by the 1st of the month. If after 30 days the rent is still unpaid, it's an additional $5 per day.

That could add up.

Also, when a tenant moves out, I assume she'll take the utilities out of her name, so I don't normally check. However, in this case, I called the electric and gas companies. She had not called them, so I asked for a copy of her most recent bill. In case she didn't pay them. I mean, her mother *had* died. Again.

Apparently, the gas company wasn't supposed to send me a copy of the bill because it was against their policy, but they did anyway. It showed her service ended June 10.

They called saying they could only send the bill to the person who pays it and asked could they please have it back.

"Sorry," I told them. "It's the only proof I have of when she moved out."

The electric company did not send me a copy of her bill.

Here's the rundown of what she owed at this point:

1. June Rent: $375.00

2. June Late Fee: $75.00

3. July Rent: $375.00

4.   July Late Fee: $75.00

Keep in mind there's an additional $5 per day per late rent month for every day after 30 days late.

If that's not incentive to pay, I don't know what is.

For three months I attempted to discover her new address. I even checked with the utility companies, but they did not find her in their records. Their verdict: "She probably has her utilities in a relative's name."

Tenant Predators do this to avoid being located.

During this time, I filed a small claim against her, but without an address, and with no forwarding address at the Post Office, it was impossible to send it to her.

We filed it anyway, to get the claim on record.

In the state in which I live, I have five years from the time a debt is incurred to file the claim.

Fast forward 4 ½ years.

I was banking at a branch I don't usually visit. As I was walking into the bank, lo and behold!, who should I encounter but my long-lost tenant of the twice-dead mother.

"Hey, hi!" I said, striking up a friendly conversation. "How's your daughter?"

She responded cheerfully. (She did not know I had a claim against her because it had never been served.)

We talked like old acquaintances do when seeing each other after several years' absence. About five minutes in, I managed, "So, where are you living now?"

She gave me a street name. It wasn't enough.

"North or south?" I asked curiously.

She answered with the exact street address.

Bingo!

Since I am generally a nice guy, I decided to send her a letter indicating she owed two month's rent and two $75 late fees: $900. I waived more than four years of late charges.

Five days later, she called me up.

"I got your letter in the mail. I don't owe rent for June or July. I moved out in April. I have the money order receipts to prove it. You're not getting your money."

Thank you, random gas company office person, for accidentally sending me her last gas bill!

I stopped by my attorney, who was aware of everything that had happened to this point.

"She's lying about her move-out date," I told him. "Let's proceed with the small claim."

"There's a $5000 cap for small claims in that apartment's county," he reminded me.

"She's claiming she owes nothing, when she knows she does. Let's take her to court for the full amount, including late fees and attorney costs."

This is the only time I chose to skip small claims and file a lawsuit in court.

The claim was as follows:

1. Past due Rent (2 Months) $750.00

2. Late Fees (first 30 days) $150.00

3. June (Over 30 Days) $5.00 * 1642 days $8,210.00

4. July (over 30 days) $5.00 * 1612 days $8,060.00

    4.1. My Claim $17,170.00

    4.2. Attorney Fees (30%) $6,868.00

5. Total Claim $24,038.00

Since this was a bench trial, she needed to be represented by an attorney, at her own expense.

For both a small claim hearing and a bench trial, the court is looking for three basic items:

1. Is there a contract or lease?

2. Is there a section of the lease the deals with attorney fees?

3. Did either party violate any portion of the contract?

A solid case needs to answer "Yes" to all three questions.

We filed the claim in June 2003, but it took two years before we won the judgment. One reason for the delay was her counter claim.

We live in a country where anyone can sue anyone else for any reason. But if a lawsuit is to hold any weight, it must be based in reality. Hers was not.

She tried suing me for $10,000 due to the "severe emotional distress" *my* claim caused her.

Here is a snapshot from the court case:

0014	06/06/2005	BT Case Decided by Bench Trial
		Comes now the court, and having taken this matter under advisement, enters the following order. Having reviewed the evidence and arguments presented, the court now enters judgment in favor of the plaintiff and against the defendant in the amount of $12,151.00. The court denies the counterclaim.
0015	06/07/2005	12151.00 Assessed JUD JUDGMENTS/GARNISHMEN

As you can see, I ended up receiving a $12,151.00 judgment (as the court felt that $16,270.00 in late fees was a bit extreme), while her claim of severe emotional distress came to nothing.

Remember, I had originally planned to waive the late charges. She could have paid $900 and been done with it. In fact, if she would have agreed to pay the past due rent of $750 only, I would have taken *that*.

Ever since I won the judgment, the past tenant had paid almost nothing against the claim. My attorney still schedules her to appear in court once a quarter to ask why.

These appearances have shown, yet again, that the tenant will lie about anything to avoid paying what she owes. In 2008, my attorney asked if she had received a tax refund for the previous year.

"No. I don't file taxes."

"Did you receive a stimulus check?" he asked. This was the year the government sent everyone a stimulus check.

"Yes."

"I will remind the court that only those who file taxes are eligible to receive a stimulus check."

The judge stepped in at this point. "Please explain how you received a stimulus check without filing a tax return?"

She had been caught.

My attorney continued: "What did you spend the stimulus money on? Remember, you are under oath."

"I needed work done on my teeth. It cost almost the whole check. It was $299, and I only received $300."

"Do you have the receipt to prove this?"

"No. I threw it away." How convenient.

"Since you have $1 remaining from the stimulus," said the judge, "you will pay that toward your claim."

Small victories.

The court allows you to charge 8% on the outstanding balance of a claim. So this is what her interest looks like since the judgment:

2007 Interest	$972.00
2008 Interest	$1049.00
2009 Interest	$1,133.00
2010 Interest	$1,224.00
2011 Interest	$1,322.00
2012 Interest	$1,428.00
2013 Interest	$1,542.00
Total Interest to Date:	$8,670.00

Someday, my past tenant is going to need a loan, and this judgment, growing year by year, is sitting on her credit report.

One moral of this experience: Even if you get a judgment in your favor, it does not mean you will collect the money in a timely manner.

I know the landlord of the unit she moved into after she left my apartment. We talk informally sometimes, giving each other a heads-up on bad tenants. That's how I found out that soon after

I received the judgment against her, she moved out of his apartment, sticking him with past due rent as well.

A second moral: Once a tenant predator, always a tenant predator.

With Real Tenant History, much of this could have been avoided. Not only can a landlord manage his properties, but he has access to thousands of tenant reviews and ratings that can wave a red flag when screening a prospective tenant.

My landlord buddy and I could have saved ourselves a lot of time and frustration with Real Tenant History.

And I wouldn't be staring at this bit of arithmetic:

Judgment:	$12,151.00
Interest:	$8,670.00
Payments:	- $251.00
Balance:	**$20,570.00**

My past tenant now lives in government subsidized housing. It's a terrible place, full of thieves, molesters, and meth heads. I cannot imagine a worse place to live.

But her rent is almost free!

7 - The Tenant Predator

What is a tenant predator?

According to Real Tenant History, a tenant predator is someone who moves from apartment to apartment every two to three months, paying very little rent or utilities.

It happens like this:

"I need a place," the person says, and he needs it now. "Can you work with me about the deposit?"

You're in the business of providing places for people to live, so you say, "Yes."

The person moves in, paying only a month, or perhaps only a week, of rent.

When the first of the month rolls around, he confesses, "I've had lots of bills lately. The rent's coming. It'll just be a little late."

You decide to check into things. You find the tenant put the utilities in his name, but he hasn't bothered to pay those either.

Mid-month rolls around. No rent. You call him up.

Excuses, excuses.

It's almost the first day of the third month since he moved in. You haven't seen the deposit money. You haven't seen the second month's rent. You draw the line: "Pay your rent in full or get out of the apartment."

"You'll have to evict me if you want me gone," he replies.

The eviction process (as you'll see in a later chapter) takes at least 30 days, and can take 60 days in some states.

When the apartment is finally rentable again, the tenant has stayed 90-120 days for the low, low price of one month's rent.

It's now that your ex-tenant repeats the process with another unsuspecting landlord. Many times, none of this activity shows up on a credit report or a background check. And if the tenant moves prior to the actual eviction hearing, it won't show up on a criminal background check either.

That's a tenant predator.

~~~

In 2002, I experienced my first tenant predator. I had been renting apartments and homes for eight years and had never seen anything like it.

I rented a three-room house to a married couple. I'll call them Fred and Jane Jones. They had three kids, all under the age of four.

The main floor had a living room, dining room, kitchen, and half-bath. Upstairs held the three bedrooms and a full bath. There was also a full basement with laundry room, work bench area, and a huge storage area. With 750 square feet per floor, it was 2,250 square feet total.

Everything was great when I showed the house. The kids were well-behaved. Fred and Jane filled the application out entirely, and all the checks I ran turned out great. When they signed the lease, they asked, "Could we pay three months' rent with the deposit?"

Three months rent in advance, I thought. *That's great!*

What I didn't consider was the time of year. It was March. To tenant predators like Fred and Jane, a tax refund is like winning the lottery, especially considering the number of children they had.

I stopped by the house during the first month because the pilot light had gone out. While I was there, I noticed they had a new sofa, a new 60" flat-screen TV, a new laptop computer, a new dining table, and a new washer and dryer.

This should have sent up red flags—living beyond their means. I would find out later it was all from a local Rent to Own.

Month two. I received a "complimentary" notice from the local water company that their bill was past due. I called Fred.

"It's being taken care of," he said.

What that meant, I found out, was that he paid $10 against the bill so that the water wouldn't be shut off.

The other utilities don't send out notices to property owners, so I didn't know the gas and electric were also overdue.

Nearly month four. Since they had not paid rent for the first three months, I decided to send an invoice reminding them rent was due June 1.

June 1 came and went without a payment. On June 2, I sent a late rent notice. A week passed. Finally, on June 9, I called. Fred answered the phone. "Hello?"

"Hi. I hope you're doing well. I was just checking in since your rent was due June 1, but I haven't seen it yet."

"Yeah, I was going to call to explain what's going on."

"I have an answering machine," I said. "I haven't received a call."

"I didn't get the answering machine when I called. I would have left a message."

"I also have caller ID. I haven't seen your number."

"I guess I had the wrong number, then."

"Okay. When do you plan on paying June's rent?"

"Work's been slow. I should have it mailed out by the 15th."

"That'll be fine. Just make sure you send in the late fee with it."

"I will. Thanks."

On the first Monday following the 15th, I went to the Post Office. The rent wasn't there. I called Fred again.

"We had to take the car to the garage. That set us back. You'll have the rent next week."

I said OK. But when I checked the next week, I found nothing. I was starting to get angry. I called again.

"We mailed a money order just today."

I wanted to be certain. "I'll stop by. I want to see the receipt for the money order."

When I arrived, no one was home. I called their cell phone, but no one answered. I went home to figure out what options I had.

The lease has the following section in it regarding "defaults."

> **DEFAULTS.** *Tenant shall be in default of this Lease if Tenant fails to fulfill any lease obligation or term by which Tenant is bound. Subject to any governing provisions of law to the contrary, if Tenant fails to cure any financial obligation within 7 days (or any other obligation within 7 days) after written notice of such default is provided by Landlord to Tenant, Landlord may take possession of the Premises without further notice (to the extent permitted by law), and without prejudicing Landlord's rights to damages. In the alternative, Landlord may elect to cure any default and the cost of such action shall be added to Tenant's financial obligations under this Lease. Tenant shall pay all costs, damages, and expenses (including reasonable attorney fees and expenses) suffered by Landlord by reason of Tenant's defaults. All sums of money or charges required to be paid by Tenant under this Lease shall be additional rent, whether or not such sums or charges are designated as "additional rent". The rights provided by this paragraph are cumulative in nature and are in addition to any other rights afforded by law.*

I called their cell phone again and told them I would be exercising the "defaults" section of their lease. They immediately returned my call and paid the rent in full, with late fees.

Since it was nearly July, I worried I would have the same issue with the July rent as with the June rent.

When July 1 came around, I check the P.O. Box. Surprise! No rent. I immediately sent out a late rent notice. I still hadn't heard anything by the 8th, which was the seven-day violation of the defaults section.

I decided to take a friend with me to the house, and we put padlocks on both the front and back doors. The tenant was locked out.

A week later, Fred called saying he had July's rent for me.

"I'll meet you at the house around 6," I said. When I met with him, I explained how things were going to go. "If rent is ever seven days or more past due, I'll put the padlocks back on."

"I understand," he said.

August. Fred called: "Work's slow. Rent will be a week late."

He had three young children and he had notified me beforehand. I told him that would be fine.

But the next week, there was still no rent. I called Fred on his cell. He didn't answer, so I left a message for him to call me back. He didn't return my call, so I put the padlocks back on.

What I didn't know was that Fred had invested in a set of bolt cutters.

I had placed the padlocks during the day. I expected a call that evening, asking me to take them off. After two days with no call, I drove by the house. They were coming and going like nothing had happened.

I called Fred yet again. "Did you happen to notice the padlocks on the doors?"

"Yes, I did. We'll not be paying rent any more. If you put the padlocks back on, I'll just cut them off."

I won't bore you with the turmoil I experienced during the eviction process. I'll just say it took me 90 days to get them out of my property. And when they finally vacated, I was not prepared for what I would find.

I have a 8'x16' trailer I use to haul items to the dump. It took four loads to clear out all the crap they left behind.

It seemed they frequented Goodwill almost every week. I found nearly 100 large trash bags full of clothing in the basement. From what I could figure, they got a bag of clothing from Goodwill, brought it home, looked through it, took what they could use, and threw the bag with the remainder down in the basement.

Another discovery I made was more disturbing. There was a small leak in the plumbing, so I decided to replace the vanity in the half-bath. I removed the screws holding it in place, unhooked the plumbing, and moved it to the living room. When I returned to the bathroom, I found more than 80 empty boxes of ephedrine where the vanity had been.

This could only mean one thing—meth.

Now, I didn't just have to clear out all their trash, I had to clean up what might have been a meth lab. Later testing showed they had not produced meth on the property, but it was still a big concern on my part at the time, never mind that they had had three children under the age of five living with them.

While I was cleaning, I noticed their car parked less than a block away at a duplex owned by a friend. I called him up. "Are you renting to Fred and Jane?"

He was. I shared my experience with him. He was mortified.

Their old unit was ready to rent after about three weeks. A nice couple moved in and lived there for years.

My friend ended up going through the same things I had. Fred and Mary vacated after about three months and moved to yet another duplex about a block from their second place.

I didn't know the landlord there, but the duplex was on Main Street, so I drove by several times a week. By now, Fred and Mary had four children. After three or four months, the duplex had a "For Rent" sign out front and Fred and Mary's car was no longer parked there.

About 15 months later, I noticed they were still living in the same area. Now they had five kids. Fred wasn't working, and word on the street was that he was manufacturing meth in the apartment basement.

As the years passed, I watched as Fred and Mary rented a number of different locations within a three block area. Some of these properties were run-down, but their options were getting slimmer and slimmer every time they moved.

Fred and Mary were finally arrested on drug charges. The oldest child was now in middle school. He was arrested multiple times for shoplifting and burglary.

Over the course of five years, Fred and Jane had lived in more than 12 different apartments.

This is what we call a tenant predator.

With Real Tenant History, you are able to scan the database to determine if a potential tenant is a tenant predator *before* you rent to him.

We never took Fred and Jane to small claims court. During the five to six months they lived on my property and the three to four months they lived at my friend's property, more than 12 businesses had filed small claims against them. These included the following:

- Wireless Provider
- Electric Company
- Gas Company
- Local Rent-to-Own Company
- Local Hospital
- Other Health Care Providers
- Prior Landlord

I would have been at the end of a very long list of people and businesses hoping to collect money from Fred and Jane.

8 - SSD and You

Renting to someone on Social Security Disability (SSD) has its own special considerations. It pays to be aware of the facts so you can protect your interests while renting to these particular tenants.

First, remember: Most people on SSD are on it for a good reason. They have legitimate disabilities that prevent them from working. They are no different than any other tenant.

Second, more and more people on SSD are renting. When I first started in 1994, I rarely had someone on SSD apply for an apartment. But in the past 10 years, I've seen the number increase dramatically. In 2014, 1 in 10 people who apply for a rental unit will list SSD as their primary source of income.

Third, some people abuse the system. And if the potential tenant abuses SSD, he will probably abuse other opportunities—such your rental unit.

Fourth, normally you just have to take the potential tenant's word on how much they are receiving from SSD.

There is a government website that shows average SSD payments for various reasons. Here's a November 2013 snapshot   from http://www.ssa.gov/policy/docs/quickfacts/stat_snapshot/:

Social Security benefits, November 2013

Type of beneficiary	Beneficiaries		Total monthly benefits (millions of dollars)	Average monthly benefit (dollars)
	Number (thousands)	Percent		
Total	57,917	100.0	67,425	1,164.18
Old-Age and Survivors Insurance	46,935	81.0	56,645	1,206.87
Retirement benefits	40,744	70.4	50,044	1,228.25
Retired workers	37,835	65.3	48,198	1,273.91
Spouses of retired workers	2,287	3.9	1,459	637.78
Children of retired workers	622	1.1	387	622.27
Survivor benefits	6,191	10.7	6,600	1,066.14
Children of deceased workers	1,891	3.3	1,515	801.23
Widowed mothers and fathers	151	0.3	137	906.06
Nondisabled widow(er)s	3,890	6.7	4,765	1,224.95
Disabled widow(er)s	257	0.4	182	706.60
Parents of deceased workers	1	(L)	1	1,077.42
Disability Insurance	10,981	19.0	10,780	981.70
Disabled workers	8,941	15.4	10,100	1,129.65
Spouses of disabled workers	157	0.3	48	303.53
Children of disabled workers	1,883	3.3	633	335.99

SOURCE: Social Security Administration, Master Beneficiary Record, 100 percent data.

Past landlord references are probably the best indicator of the applicant's honesty and reliability. Using Real Tenant History will give you the necessary information from past landlords.

In addition to seeing the applicant's Tenant Information Landlord Evaluation (TILE) score, you can also see if he has been deemed a Tenant Predator.

As mentioned in the previous chapter, a tenant predator is someone who moves from apartment to apartment every two-three months without paying for utilities and paying little to no rent.

If a tenant falls into the tenant predator area, you should avoid renting to him at all costs.

A final thing to keep in mind when renting to a tenant on SSD is that if you ever need to send them to small claims court, you will be unable to receive a penny from their SSD. That's how the law works.

If that makes you nervous about renting to such a tenant, here's one solution: make sure the tenant has a cosigner.

This gives you an alternative source for collection of any outstanding invoices that may arise if the tenant fails to meet his financial commitments.

Also, the cosigner will normally know where the tenant lives after moving out, so it will be easier to track him down if the tenant still owes rent or needs to finish clean-up.

If you keep these tips in mind, you'll be able to safely and effectively rent to many good tenants who happen to be on SSD.

9 - The Alpha Dog

In 2011, I rented to a single woman who was about seven months pregnant. She worked at a local daycare; everything checked out on her application.

When she looked at the apartment and signed the lease, her boyfriend was also there. "Would it be OK if he stays with me?" she asked.

"Sure."

The boyfriend was what you would call an Alpha Dog. He was outspoken. He gave commands. And she always submitted to his commands.

When something needed done at the apartment--the lawn mowed or the dumpster emptied or an outside light bulb changed—he called me and *told me* what needed done. Now.

An Alpha Dog is a bully. He tells you what to do and how to do it. He brags about his own performance (which is probably average) and criticizes yours. He takes credit for other people's ideas and likes to take charge, even if he isn't in a leadership position.

Romanticize humanity as much as you like, but I argue we share a great deal with our furry four-legged friends. I have a friend who watches *The Dog Whisperer* for tips on managing his kids' behavior. And you know what--it works.

Bullies are basically dogs with behavioral problems that have been allowed to run amok. Understanding that can help you survive, and thrive, when interacting with an Alpha Dog.

Here's how the Alpha Dog acts. He growls and expects the other dogs to back away. Any dog that doesn't back away, gets a set of jaws around his neck until he submits.

What you need to do to work with an Alpha Dog is to determine what his ego needs. Does it need flattery? Reliability? A willingness to stay late? Whatever it is, give it to them.

I hate to say it, but if you can learn to fake sincerity with such a person, it'll make your life much easier.

And so, this young woman's boyfriend was an Alpha Dog. He was always right (even if he said something stupid). But since he wasn't on the lease, I didn't give much weight to what he was saying.

Sometimes when he called about some work that needed done, I told him his girlfriend needed to call, since the lease was between me and her.

This did not sit well with him. He felt I was undermining his authority.

Two months into the lease, the tenant gave birth to a healthy baby boy. She planned to take 12 weeks off because of the Family and Medical Leave Act (FMLA) to take care of her new baby.

Things remained good. Rent was always prompt. Issues were communicated directly. There was only one wrinkle. The woman insisted that if I needed to stop by the apartment, I had to wait until her boyfriend was home. There seemed to be a trust issue between my tenant and her boyfriend.

Six months into the lease, the boyfriend called to say they would be moving at the end of the month.

"My tenant signed a one-year lease," I tried to explain.

"The lease does not specifically say we have to stay for the entire time of the lease," he argued. "So we can move whenever we want to."

"I really need to talk to my tenant," I said. "The lease is between me and her. I need to discuss this with her."

"We're moving out at the end of the month. There's nothing you can do about it."

"It's true, I can't force you to stay, but your girlfriend will be responsible for early termination of the lease. She'll continue to be billed for rent until I find a suitable tenant to move in."

He then told me to do something I don't think is physically possible. Also, they would not be paying any more rent. Oh, and they expected their deposit back in full.

I said good-bye as politely as I could and hung up.

Now it was time for the real work to begin.

When the end of the month came, I went over to the apartment. It was relatively clean. There was some damage to repair and general cleaning to do.

Then I created a Termination of Tenancy Report using the tools provided by Real Tenant History. Here it is:

Security Deposit Notice to Tenant - Termination of Tenancy

Forwarding Address:

Sent June 10th, 2013

You must respond to this notice by mail within 7 days
after receipt of same, otherwise you will forfeit the
amount claimed for damages.

On or about _ June 1st, 2013_____, your occupancy of the premises commomly known as
_____ terminated pursuant to statute,
this notice is given to advise you of the items charged against your security deposit
as follows:

(A)	Rent Deposit		$350.00
(B)	Pet Deposit $_____ Less $_____ (Non Refundable)		
(C)	Key Deposit		$0
(D)	Net Deposit Refundable		($350.00)

Tenant Moved without notifying Landlord after 7 days

CHARGES AGAINST SECURITY DEPOSIT

	Cost to Repair/Replace
1. Carpet Cleaning (Phend' Carpet Cleaning $146.29)	$ 146.29
2. Clean Fridge (Moldy) - 2 Hours @ $25.00	$ 50.00
3. Replace Fridge Brackets for Door Shelves (4 Brackets) $35.57 + 1 hr	$ 60.57
4. Replace Back Door Blind ($49.99 + 1 Hour Labor @ $25)	$ 74.99
5. Fix Hole in Wall	$ 75.00
6. Fix Whole behind front door (While Occupying Apartment)	$ 75.00
7. Paint Walls due to cleanliness (6 Hours + 5 Gallons Paint)	$ 299.00
8. Clean Tub and Toilet (2 Hours)	$ 50.00
9. General Cleaning (3 Hours @ $25.00)	$ 75.00

(E)	Total Damages			$905.85
(F)	Unpaid Rent	May 2013 through October 2013)		$ 2,100.00
(G)	Other Charges	*Rent Through end of Lease		
		Court Charges	$92.00	
		Late Fees	$ 150.00 May/June Late Fees	
		Late Fees	$ -	
		Other	$_____ Explain _____	$242.00
(H)	Total Charges against security deposit		(E) plus (F) plus (G)	$3,247.85
(I)	Refund of Rent From _____ to _____ @ $____ per day			$0.00

BALANCE

If Positive Balance Due You *** Check Enclosed ***
If Negative-Amount Due us *** **Please pay within 7 days *** If Payment**
Matter will be turned over to our Attorney.

Remit Payment to

Date: _____   Signed by: _____

When the boyfriend saw the report, he was outraged. "You won't see a penny of it!" he said. "If you take us to small claims, we'll win."

I wouldn't take "them" to court. As I'd said so many times before, the lease was between me and the young lady.

I proceeded with the small claims process (see Appendix). What follows are the court fees and judgment. I did, indeed, see more than a "penny of it."

Due Date	Description			Judgment Amount	Paid
	100 ST COURT COSTS			$24.50	$24.50
	9/4/2013	#43675	NON LOCAL CHECK		$24.50
	116 ARK-ST			$5.00	$5.00
	9/4/2013	#43675	NON LOCAL CHECK		$5.00
	123 JUDICIAL INS ADJ FEE			$1.00	$1.00
	9/4/2013	#43675	NON LOCAL CHECK		$1.00
	125 PUBLIC DEFENSE ADMIN			$5.00	$5.00
	9/4/2013	#43675	NON LOCAL CHECK		$5.00
	126 COURT ADMIN FEE			$5.00	$5.00
	9/4/2013	#43675	NON LOCAL CHECK		$5.00
	127 JUDICIAL SALARIES FEE			$15.00	$15.00
	9/4/2013	#43675	NON LOCAL CHECK		$15.00
	130 PRO BONO LEGAL SERV			$1.00	$1.00
	9/4/2013	#43675	NON LOCAL CHECK		$1.00
	200 CO COURT COSTS			$9.45	$9.45
	9/4/2013	#43675	NON LOCAL CHECK		$9.45
	205 CITY COURT COSTS			$1.05	$1.05
	9/4/2013	#43675	NON LOCAL CHECK		$1.05
	216 DOCUMENT STORAGE FEE			$2.00	$2.00
	9/4/2013	#43675	NON LOCAL CHECK		$2.00
	217 ARK-CO CLERK PEP			$2.00	$2.00
	9/4/2013	#43675	NON LOCAL CHECK		$2.00
	222 SMALL CLAIMS SERVICE			$10.00	$10.00
	9/4/2013	#43675	NON LOCAL CHECK		$81.00	$81.00
10/29/2013	501 TRUST-D2 JUDGMENTS			$2939.39	$0.00
				$2939.39	$0.00

There are two lessons here. One: know who your tenant is and who it isn't.

And two: just because someone thinks he knows the law, it does not mean he actually does. Even if he barks really loud.

10 - Collecting Rent

Should you charge rent weekly or monthly?

To answer that, we need to examine the costs and time associated with both options.

Many people think that by charging rent weekly you can actually make more. The math goes like this: There are 12 months in a year; each month consists of 4 weeks; therefore, monthly rent nets you 48 weeks of payment. By charging weekly rent, however, you get 52 weeks of rent—that's a whole extra month of money!

Let's look at the differences more closely, though. Assume you have three rental properties, each with two units, for a total of six units. Also, let's assume weekly rent is due on Saturday and monthly rent is due on the 1st of the month.

Now, with that set-up, let's ask a few questions:

- How do you collect rent?

- Are you charging and tracking late fees?

- How much of your time is required to collect rent?

- Are you making daily, weekly, or monthly deposits?

There are many ways to collect rent, three primary ways are — through the mail, through a dropbox, or in person.

If your tenants send rent in by mail, then it must be postmarked by the due date to avoid being late. If a payment is late, you have to charge and manage late fees. This takes time. If rent is weekly, you have to process mail weekly.

Here's a possible breakdown of the time involved:

- 1 hour spent/week   4.25 hours/month

- 1 hour spent/month   1 hour/month

Now, if you have a drop box for collecting rent, you'll need to check and process the drop box daily to ensure the date rent was received. Let's throw that into the mix:

- ½ hour spent/day   11 hour/month

If you decide to collect rent in person, that opens a different can of worms. Not only is it probably the most time-consuming method of collecting rent, it requires the tenants to be home when you stop by to collect rent. And if they aren't home, it's not necessarily their fault rent is late. They can claim you didn't show up at the time you specified. It becomes your word against theirs. More than that, it's now completely your responsibility, as landlord, to collect the rent.

We'll add this option in anyway:

- Weekly - 15 minutes/unit x 6 units = 1 ½ hours/week = 5 hours/month

- Monthly - 15 minutes/unit x 6 units = 1 ½ hours/month

As they say, time is money. Your time is worth at least $25/hour, unless you want to sell yourself short. So when you start adding up the "cost" of collecting rent, weekly rent shows its true colors.

Say your tenants mail in rent, the most time-efficient method we've examined. Look at the difference in cost:

Weekly rent collection cost for six units:

- 4.25 hours x $25 = $106.26

Monthly rent collection cost for six units:

- 1.50 Hours x 25 = $37.50

These are only the costs of rent collection. If we add in the time it takes to charge and manage late fees, the cost continues to rise.

It's obvious that monthly rent saves the landlord money.

But what about our earlier problem, the difference between 48 weeks of rent (monthly) and 52 weeks of rent (weekly)? The easy answer—take the difference into account.

Say we charge a weekly rent of $95-$105 on a one-bedroom apartment. The monthly charge should be between $410 and $455. Or, in other words, the total weekly rent for a year of use divided by 12 months.

This way you'll be collecting the same amount in rent while cutting your administration costs by 300%.

Because, really, no one goes into the Independent Rental Owner business because he wants to be a collection agent. Whatever your reason, I'm certain it wasn't so you could run around and collect rent.

And if it was, well, be my guest. Collect rent weekly. In person.

As for me, collecting monthly allows me more time to spend on the 20% that matters.

11 - The Cover Charge

Collecting rent in person has its downsides. It takes extra time, the tenant might not be home, and sometimes you have to pick it up from the tenant's place of employment.

That can be awkward. I know from experience.

A few years back, two women rented from me. When they filled out their applications, they entered "LNG Investments" as their employer and "entertainer" as their job description. They had a letter from their employer indicating their weekly take-home pay. Since they were 1099 employees, they didn't have paystubs to show.

I didn't think anything of it at the time.

One of the tenants, Cindy, signed a lease that required a weekly rent payment. I stopped by the apartment once a week to pick it up, and the rent was always on time and paid in full.

But one week I stopped at my regular time and no one was home. I didn't want to waste my trip, so I texted Cindy to see where she was.

She texted back that she had been called into work to fill in for a sick co-worker.

"Could you stop by LNG to pick up the rent?" she texted.

I said I would. When I arrived at her place of employment, I discovered what LNG stood for--Live Nude Girls.

I filled out the receipt in the car so I could spend as little time inside as possible.

At the front door, the doorman stopped me. "There's a $5 cover charge."

"I'm not here for that. I'm here to pick up rent. I'm just going in and out real quick."

"It's $5 if you want to enter."

"Look, I just need to see Cindy for a moment. Can you get her for me?"

"We don't have any Cindys working this evening. Are you sure that's her stage name?"

Oddly enough, I had never thought to ask my tenant her stage name.

"I just need to collect rent and then I'll be gone."

"If you want to enter, you need to pay the cover charge."

This was getting nowhere. I already had an hour invested in collecting this week's rent, so I broke down and paid the cover charge.

Inside, I decided to text Cindy to find out where she was.

After a couple minutes of waiting uncomfortably, she texted she was in the back.

I weaved my way through the other entertainers, who kept offering private dances.

I just wanted to get my rent and leave.

Cindy saw me first and walked up to me in her "work outfit." This is not how you expect to meet your tenant. Ever.

She handed me the weekly rent, mostly in ones and fives. (Go figure.) I counted the money to double check the amount.

"You staying for the show?" she asked. "I'm on stage next."

I guess she wanted to get some of her money back. "Some other time, perhaps." I handed her the receipt and left.

Never to return.

12 - Nice Guys Finish . . . Where, Again?

Some tenants are just plain nice. They greet you, they smile. They like to have a conversation with you. They never complain, or if some repair or issue does come up, they take it in stride. They're patient and understanding and, really, who wouldn't want more tenants who are just, well, *pleasant*?

Pleasant tenants make you want to go above and beyond the call of duty. You want to make sure everything's working out for them.

And then—*wham!* While you're being the "nice guy," they take advantage of you. It happens more often than I'd like to admit.

For instance, I had a nice family of four renting a four-bedroom house. They'd been there about six months, two unmarried adults and the man's two sons.

It was December when I received the call. "I wanted to tell you I'm expecting in January," the woman told me. "I hope the new addition won't be a problem."

"No, of course not. It won't be an issue at all. Thank you for informing me, though."

January came. I received rent on the 1st as usual. She gave birth toward the end of January. Everything seemed fine.

When February rolled around and I checked the mail--no rent. I decided to call.

"We've had some unexpected bills," the man said. "Rent's going to be a couple weeks late."

"Okay," I said, "that'll be fine, but you'll have to pay the $75 late fee as well." Many times I'll waive the late fee as long as I receive notice prior to the first of the month that rent is going to be late. But since they hadn't given me the heads up, the late fee was a good warning.

I checked the post office again mid-month—still no rent. This time I decided to stop by the house. I knew the family was going through lots of changes, but I wanted to stay informed.

The man of the house was in. "Work's slowed down," he said. "I'm sorry. It's just been rough lately."

"Okay," I told him. "But get it to me ASAP."

Now, the lease is very specific when it comes to late fees:

LATE PAYMENTS. Tenant shall pay a late fee equal to $75.00 for each payment that is not paid by the due date (1st of every month). Additional $5.00 per day late fee for all payments over <u>30 days</u> late. Deposit may not be used for last month's rent.

When the end of February rolled around, I called the tenant again. I got yet another excuse. "Don't worry," he said. "Rent's coming the first of March."

The family had a new baby, two boys in middle school, and the mother was now on maternity leave. The father was the only source of income. I knew things were tight.

Plus, it was winter. They had other bills, such as electric, gas, water, and sewer. I always try not to remove a tenant during the winter months if I can help it.

But as you might have guessed, when March arrived I still had no rent. I decided not to bother him and give him until the next Monday. But when I checked the mail again—surprise, surprise—no rent.

At this point, he owed two months of rent, two $75 late fees, and the $5 per day late fee for being more than 30 days overdue.

I called the tenant again.

"We're sorry. We have a money order we were just getting ready to mail out."

"That'll be great."

So the next Monday I went to the Post Office. As promised, there was the money order. There was one problem—it was only for $100. He conveniently forgot to mention that.

Their rent wasn't out of line for the area in which they were living. One month was $695. Add the $75 late fee, and it came to $770. With the $100 payment, they still owed $1440. And the March rent was nearly due.

I felt bad for them. I did. I decided to visit and discuss with them ways we could work together so they could get caught up on their rent.

Here's what the situation looked like:

• January	$595.00	$75.00	+ $5.00/day over 30 days
• February	$695.00	$75.00	+ $5.00/day over 30 days
• March	$695.00	$75.00	Not over 30 days yet!
	$1,985.00	$225.00	$505.00
	Total Due: $2,715.00		

By now it was nearly March 15th and they were behind almost $3000. Even so, I felt obligated to help out because of the newborn and the stress that places on a family. I tried not to worry about the possibility of the debt remaining unpaid forever.

We came to an agreement that they would pay $200 a week, which I would pick up every Saturday. This was a big step forward.

Five steps, to be exact. After the fifth week, the plan fell apart.

For two weeks in a row, no one was home when I stopped by. I couldn't help but feel they were avoiding me.

I sent a certified letter indicating that if they did not pay a substantial portion of what was owed, I had no option but to refuse to renew their lease in June.

The payments began again until June 6. By that time, their lease had auto-renewed for three-months because they had continued to make payments. Here are my renewal terms:

RENEWAL TERMS. *This Lease shall automatically renew for an additional period of 3 Months per renewal term, unless either party gives written notice of the termination no later than 30 days prior to the end of the term or renewal term. The lease terms during any such renewal term shall be the same as those contained in this Lease.*

I had not given them 30 days' notice, so I didn't have the choice to let the lease lapse. (I would not let that happen again in such a situation!)

Now that the lease had been renewed, the payments stopped. I received no rent at all during June or July. Again, I sent a certified letter stating their lease would expire at the end of August unless rent was up to date.

In no time, the man of the house brought me a $1000 money order just before the last 30 days of their lease.

"You're still $2000 short," I told him. "As long as that's paid before the end of your lease, I'll renew it."

As the end of the month approached, I received two phone calls from housing complexes. They were looking for a reference.

"The tenant is behind on rent for more than $4000," I told them truthfully. I doubted either complex would rent to a tenant with that sort of reference.

At the end of the month, I still had not heard from the tenant. I decided to visit the property. Here's what I found:

Kitchen

Kitchen

Fridge

Kids' Bedroom

Stove

Kitchen

I was extremely unhappy with what I found. I called the cell numbers I had on file.

No answer.

I tried every day for a week.

Voice mail. Every time. I never received a return call.

I moved their belongings into the living room while I cleaned, scrubbed, painted, and made repairs. Since this was a four-bedroom house, it took two weeks to complete everything.

Still, no contact with the tenant.

Once the property was ready for carpet cleaning, which is the tenant's responsibility upon move-out, I dumped their belongings.

Three pick-up loads. Forty-five dollars a load, plus labor.

Finally, the place was ready to rent again—after losing a month's rent during the time it took to clean it up.

Unfortunately, trying to help a tenant out doesn't always work in your favor. I've gone out of my way to work with tenants a couple times over the past 20 years. Based on this last experience, I don't think I'll do so again.

On the following page is the "Termination of Tenancy" report created using Real Tenant History. It simplified the process of submitting our small claims with the attorney.

Security Deposit Notice to Tenant - Termination of Tenancy

Forwarding Address.

Sent November 26, 2013

You must respond to this notice by mail within 7 days
after receipt of same, otherwise you will forfeit the
amount claimed for damages.

On or about _ November 1st, 2013_____, your occupancy of the premises commomly known
_____, Kendallville, IN 46755 terminated pursuant to statute,
this notice is given to advise you of the items charged against your security deposit
as follows:

(A)	Rent Deposit	$695.00
(B)	Pet Deposit $_____ Less $_____ (Non Refundable)	
(C)	Key Deposit	$0
(D)	Net Deposit Refundable	($695.00)

Tenant Moved without notifying Landlord after 7 days

CHARGES AGAINST SECURITY DEPOSIT — Cost to Repair/Replace

CHARGES AGAINST SECURITY DEPOSIT	Cost to Repair/Replace
1. Wash/Repair and Paint Walls (18.5 Hours)	$ 462.50
2. Remove 3 Truck Loads of Items left behind	$ 300.00
3. General Cleaning (15 Hours @ 25.00)	$ 375.00
4. Repalce Blinds and missing light covers	$ 252.00
5.	$ 63.00
6.	
7.	
8.	
9.	

(E)	Total Damages	$1,452.50
(F)	Unpaid Rent Multiple Months	$ 3,675.00
(G)	Other Charges	

Court Charges	$104.00	Two People
Late Fees	$ 450.00	6 Months Late Fees
Attorney Fees:		* Attorney Fees at 40% of Claim

	Other	$____	Explain	_____	$554.00
(H)	Total Charges against security deposit			(E) plus (F) plus (G)	$5,681.50

(I)	Refund of Rent From _____ to _____ @ $_____ per day	$0.00

BALANCE   (D) minus (H) Plus (I) ($4,986.50)

If Positive Balance Due You *** Check Enclosed ***
If Negative-Amount Due us *** **Please pay within 7 days *** If Payment not received within 7 days, this
Matter will be turned over to our Attorney.**

Remit Payment to .

Date: _____   Signed by: _____

My attorney sent a certified letter to the house address, which was forwarded to the tenant's new address. He refused the letter.

Next, I had the sheriff's department serve the notice to the man's place of employment. This is usually my last resort. No one likes to be served by the sheriff at work.

As of the writing of this chapter, the small claim is still pending.

13 - 81 Reasons Rent is Late

Late rent is a fact of being a landlord, and with late rent comes all kinds of excuses. What follows, in no particular order, are some of the common (and not so common) excuses we've heard over our years as landlords.

And, yes, these have all actually been used.

1. "My work cut my hours."
2. "My pay week is off this month."
3. "I've been really sick this past week."
4. "The bank mailed the check to the wrong address."
5. "My daughter got married and I had to pay for the wedding."
6. "My sister passed away this weekend. Can I call you back?"
7. "My car was stolen."
8. "My nephew was shot in the head and we had to pull the plug on him this past weekend."
9. "Someone hit me across both knees with a baseball bat at work and I've been in the hospital."
10. "I fell over a wheelchair at work and hit my head. I was in a coma the last few days."
11. "My mother died." (For the second time.)
12. "I usually get $25 a blow job, but I haven't given many this month."
13. "My food stamp card is missing."
14. "My boss's bank was shut down, so it'll take an extra week to process the checks."
15. "Sorry, I just spent the rent on my honeymoon."
16. "Our illegal roommate skipped out on us, so we don't have the money."
17. "I know I didn't pay the last couple months. I'll pay next month, I promise. Can you let me back in now?"
18. "My drug habit keeps getting in the way!"

19. "I know rent is due on the first, but I already spent the money from my last check. I'll pay it when I get my next check."
20. "I get paid bi-weekly and my check is mailed from Washington. Currently they are having an anthrax problem and all mail will be held up indefinitely."
21. "I needed to buy food this month."
22. "I have to spend it on my dying grandmother. My mum and dad died a long time ago and I'm the only daughter. Also, last time I paid the rent, my grandfather died! So, please, I'll pay the rent when my grandmother dies."
23. "I left the money for rent and the money for groceries in two different envelopes. My boyfriend must have taken the wrong one, so this will have to do for now."
24. "My bank closed my account and didn't tell me. That's why the check bounced."
25. "I spent it all on Christmas presents for the kids. You don't expect me to tell my kids they don't get Christmas presents, do you?"
26. "I'm not paying my rent this month because the bathtub overflowed and it ruined my brand new TV."
27. "I'm not paying this month because I'm moving out next month. You just keep my security deposit for this month's rent."
28. "I haven't paid my rent because I don't have any money!"
29. "I ran out of stamps to mail it." –from letter mailed in a stamped envelope.
30. "I don't feel like paying it."
31. "I haven't paid my rent because I was hardly home this past month and I probably won't be home much this month, either."
32. "The reason I didn't pay the rent before the end of my 72-hour termination notice was because I was in jail."
33. "I didn't pay my rent because five of the fifteen hallway lights were burned out."
34. "I didn't pay my rent because the knob on a closet door is inoperable."
35. "My car was repossessed and my paycheck was in it."

36. "My boyfriend's parents are giving us a house to live in for free, so I'm moving out. So I'm not paying this month's rent, but I'll do you a favor and let you use my full security deposit for the entire month, even though we'll be leaving in two weeks. Oh, by the way, there's a problem with the kitchen stove. It's not been working right for a real long time. And last night there was this little fire."

37. "I'm a sick person. I need money for prescriptions this month."

38. "Here's half the rent. I can't live here any more. My roommates are running a meth lab in the bathroom." —a lie she told when she was going to move out with her sperm donor. Luckily, the roommates had already paid the rent.

39. "My husband just got a new job and will be out of town for three weeks. I know what the contract says. Please don't evict us. I have four children."

40. "The weather's been bad so work's been slow. Check is in the mail."

41. "My wife is in the hospital with heart problems. She almost had a heart attack." A week later, the wife

explains she almost had a stress-induced heart attack because they can't pay the rent.

42. "We're waiting to get the settlement from the lawyer. We told him we just want five million, but he wants to drag it out and try for ten. We'll call you after we meet with him."

43. "Our roommates paid half the first month then said the following month, 'Oh, we thought you were taking care of this month's and we would pay half of next month's.' Needless to say they're not on the lease so we're kicking them out."

44. "I can't pay you in regular money, but I was wondering if I could pay with Monopoly money."

45. "I got a phone call from my dead mother telling me that after thinking it over she decided she never intended me to get the apartment so there won't be rent until I get another call from her telling me it's OK."

46. "I can't pass up a challenge, and it's a real challenge to see how long the rent balance can go up before I get the notices, and then to see how many notices I can defer with a variety of excuses."

47. "My astrologer told me that due to Mercury going retrograde today, it was not advisable to send in the rent. Even though it is supposed to go direct next month, Venus and Mars will be going retrograde and the Venus retrograde will cause my roommate and lover to walk out, leaving me stuck with his portion, and then the Mars retrograde will probably cause a major blow up at work, causing job loss and thus no rent for the next few months."

48. "You haven't fixed anything in the apartment that you promised me in my lease. I'll be moving soon, so keep my deposit."

49. "Dear sir, I cannot pay my rent this month because my check was a little short this week. I will pay next week."

50. "I can't pay the rent on time this month because I was laid-off and my total monthly income from unemployment is just enough to pay the rent with enough left over to pay something on another bill and

buy a little food. But since a $100 late charge and a $38 court filing fee were added to last month's rent and I paid that, it's backed me up a couple weeks. It's really hard to live on $15 a month."

51. "My supervisor failed to put in my timecard. Therefore, I didn't get a check on the 1st like expected, but I'll receive two checks on the 15th because of the supervisor's screw up. I'll pay you then."

52. "My cousin is in jail/is getting married/just died/is in the hospital and I had to help him out this month. I'll have the rest of the rent in two weeks."

53. "Rent was two weeks late because the lawnmower broke, and we had to fix it because we know you hate it when the lawn gets too long." This property had a lawn service that did the mowing.

54. "I can't send a payment in today or anytime soon because I have more important bills."

55. "My ex-husband wiped out all of my accounts and my attorney stopped payment on all my checks." The rent check had a "stop payment" on it when I went to cash it

56. "I spent all my money to put my niece in rehab. She's strung out on ice." Then: "I have the money, but it's Labor Day and the bank is closed, so I'll have it to you tomorrow." Next day, no rent. Now he tells me: "The IRS put a freeze on all my bank accounts." Three excuses in two days!

57. "My ex quit paying child support. I'll pay you after I take him to court."

58. "I can only give you a third of the rent from now on because of the unwelcome guest I have that has decided to pull the money off of the dresser and take it into the walls."

59. "Just a second. Let me turn off the lights." When the tenant did, cockroaches appeared. "Well, Mr. Landlord, I have my half of the rent. Do you have yours? You never told me I would be having breakfast, lunch, and dinner guests. I need reimbursement for other occupants that like to come out and play in the wee hours of the night.

Now that I think about it, I don't need to pay all the rent because they're here more than I am."

60. "The IRS has seized all my assets."

61. "I had to take my sick dog to the vet and the X-ray showed that he ate a large piece of carpet in the living room. The bill is up over $800 and I already paid them the $600 that I had set aside for rent this month. I'll have it for you in a week. My mom is sending me money." I told her: "Please include the nonrefundable pet deposit that I told you would be owed if you had a dog in my rental house." No pets were allowed in the house. "Also I need to come by and estimate the damage the dog did to the carpet in the living room." She began crying harder and hung up. She moved before I could even stop by and check out the damage to the carpet.

62. "I taught my daughter that money is dirty and you shouldn't play with it. So I can't pay my rent because my toddler just flushed the rent down the toilet."

63. "I am so sorry that I am late paying my rent this month. I fell in the shower, hit my head, and subsequently forgot what month it was. Do you need a doctor's note?"

64. "I don't know why you expect a full month's rent when since the beginning I haven't paid it in full. And you've never fixed the shower. I can live with that if you can live with getting only $300 this time. I promise next pay check you'll get some more. I don't think you have the balls to kick me out anyway. I mean, are you really gonna find someone else to live in this dump? No!"

65. "I'm having problems with the timing belt in my truck. It'll cost me $600. I also just found out that if I don't pay the IRS $300 per month starting with a $300 deposit, my pay will be garnished in full until I've paid everything in full. My rent is $900, so there you go."

66. "Didn't you get the letter from my attorney stating that you two"—the leasing consultant and the manager—"are fired? I own this property and I don't have to pay rent. But you need to pay me for using my office." This tenant believed she owned the property.

67. "I had to pay for my INS Green Card renewal." –from a tenant with a five-year history of late rent.
68. "I can't pay rent until the middle of the month because I had to bail myself out of jail." –new tenant who had passed a background check.
69. "My dog needs a rabies shot. If I don't get him one, he could bite someone and you could be sued." –a tenant with three dogs in a no-dog apartment. Also, even if the shot is $50, what happened to the other $950?
70. "I was on my way to town to pay you rent, but my bag fell out of the car with $800 in it. I guess someone got an early Christmas present."
71. "We were at an amusement park and the rent money was in my pocket. It all fell out on the rollercoaster."
72. "We were at a parade. Our car was broken into and my wife's purse was stolen. The rent money ($1025 cash) was in it."
73. "I came to drop it off and you weren't home."
74. "My boyfriend moved back in with his wife, and I lost my job."
75. "I was overpaid by Social Security for my deceased husband, so they are taking the amount overpaid out of my 16-year-old son's Social Security check. He will only get $16 for November."
76. "We are waiting for our tax refund to come."
77. "As soon as my son moves in, I'll get caught up." One month later: "As soon as my best friend moves in, I'll get caught up."
78. "My wife went to deposit my paycheck, but the computers were down at Bank of America."
79. "My boss is having financial trouble and hasn't paid me yet."
80. "My student loan got taken out of my last check by mistake. When the money is refunded to me, you'll get your rent."

And, of course:
81. "I just plum forgot!"

14 - The Squatter

According to dictionary.com, a squatter is "a person who settles on land or occupies property without title, right, or payment of rent."

So, if you have a squatter, it makes sense to kick them out.

Sorry. You can't. It's not that easy.

According to the law, as a property owner, you have to treat these people the same way you treat paying tenants. It's not right, it doesn't make sense, but there it is.

I'll explain.

This will not cut it if you want to keep squatters out.

First, let's look at some examples of squatting.

Imagine after three long months away, you're finally home. It was a rough trip, but now you're at your front door. You step inside.

Something's wrong.

The lights are on. There's a bag of chips open on the coffee table. A bath towel is draped over the back of the armchair.

Adrenaline courses through your body—a burglar's been here.

Then a guy wanders into the room. He's wearing your robe.

"Who're you?" he asks.

You look everything over one more time. Yes, yes, this is your place. That's all your stuff. But someone else is using it.

Friend, you've got yourself a squatter.

The International Squatter's Symbol

Squatting's pretty simple. You set up camp on land or in a house. If people live there, it's home invasion. If people don't, it's squatting.

People squat for lots of different reasons. The poverty-stricken commonly build shantytowns on property they don't own. The homeless may take refuge in an abandoned home for a few nights—or a few years. Political types squat to make a statement about the economic gap between rich and poor. And sometimes squatting's just a way to buck authority.

Even a houseguest who refuses to leave is considered a squatter, as is the tenant who stays after his lease expires.

We have property rights here in the US (thank you forefathers!), so squatters have the law to contend with, but there are still plenty of legal loopholes squatters take advantage of.

So while the life of a squatter is fraught with pitfalls and confrontations, so is the life of the landlord who has to deal with such illegal residents. There are laws that give rights to squatters as well as a process for landowners to get rid of them.

The question, then, is how exactly does squatting work, legally?

The key to successful squatting lies in a tenant's rights. States grant certain rights to people who live in a home they do not own. These rights protect tenants from being kicked out without notice.

In most states, tenant rights are extended to anyone living in a home for a certain period of time, usually 30 days or more.

Squatters exploit these rights. By making repairs, adding curtains, and performing other actions that show one settling into the home in a respectable manner, the appearance of tenant's rights are established.

In time, squatters can even earn ownership of the house. There's legal precedent in the US called adverse possession. This states that if a squatter lives "openly, continuously, and hostilely" in a home for a prescribed number of years, he can become the owner of that house.

As long as the squatter makes no attempts to hide his habitation (openly), stays there continuously, and stays without permission (hostilely), he can take possession when the time limit is reached, as long as he also pays the property taxes on the house.

Another truth of squatting is that, one way or another, a squatter is going to be visited by the police. Neighbors may call the authorities, or a landlord may drop by and find unwanted tenants on one of his properties.

If police find squatters, there's not much they can do. Police uphold criminal law, not civil law. Civil law is worked out in the courts.

Once police determine a squatter has established some sort of tenancy, it becomes a civil matter. And if the squatter has set up house in a generally respectable manner, the appearance of tenant's rights can confound a clean-cut case.

If a squatter sets up utilities, a process which generally doesn't require proof of tenantship, he now has enough evidence of residency for police in some cities. It is now the landlord's responsibility to prove in court the squatter doesn't belong in the house. And once the court has the case, it can take years to resolve.

Luckily, my personal experience with a squatter didn't go this far.

I have a fourplex with a basement that is accessible by all the tenants because the breaker boxes are there and in case of tornadoes.

In the first month of winter, I received a phone call from one of the downstairs tenants asking if I had someone storing items in the basement.

"No," I said.

"Well, there's a man moving items down there in the evenings."

I decided to investigate.

It didn't take long to figure out someone had taken up residence in my basement. The space isn't rentable; it's a "common area" at best.

The squatter had moved into the back portion so as to avoid being noticed by the casual observer. He had already moved in a twin bed, blankets, pillows, a few plastic tubs with personal belongings, a radio, and a small TV with rabbit-ears. A 20' x 30' tarp covered the floor.

He had also cut a few holes in the heating vents heading to the apartments and had a bucket next to the overflow valve from the water heater. Amenities, heat, hot water. He was set.

The squatter was gone when I arrived and discovered his living area. I called the police. This was not a rentable unit, so he was trespassing. Therefore, it *was* a criminal case instead of a civil issue in this instance. But I couldn't pursue the case further until I found my squatter.

I talked to all the tenants and asked them to call me when they saw him return.

A few days later, about 10 pm, I received a phone call from the tenant who originally informed me of the squatter. He was back.

I drove over to the property, arranging for the local police to join me.

When we arrived, the police entered the basement first, and I followed. Since there was only one way in and out, there was no way he could slip out unnoticed.

The police found him lying in his bed, watching TV.

"What are you doing?" they asked.

"What does it look like? I'm watching TV. I live here. I rent this place."

The lie didn't last long.

"This man here owns the apartment," the police said, indicating me. "He informed us he had a squatter in his basement. We're going to have to ask you to leave and take your belongings with you."

"We can arrange a time for you to pick up what you can't take at the moment," I added.

He left, and I never received a call from him to pick up the rest of his stuff.

After this, I put locks and deadbolts on all property basements that are considered "common areas." Tenants are given keys to these areas if they need routine access.

Although I had no drawn-out confrontation with the squatter, I did have to repair his "modifications," which cost me a few hundred dollars.

Although I would call the man setting up house in my basement a "real" squatter, any tenant who is not paying his rent is technically a squatter. These cases, though, are not solved as quickly.

This is one reason we developed Real Tenant History. We want to ensure every landlord has the tools for tracking and documenting tenants. Using the ratings and reviews, landlords can avoid renting to a known squatter.

It's better to catch a squatter before he can put down roots.

15 - Those Wonderful Kids

About 10 years ago, I showed an upstairs two-bedroom apartment to a woman, Linda. The features were fantastic: two full baths, two bedrooms, a laundry room with washer and dryer, a spacious kitchen, a large living room, two walk-in closets, off-street parking, and a yard. All this on a quiet street close to downtown.

Linda immediately fell in love with it. She spent about an hour going through the apartment, filling out the application, and asking a bunch of questions. They were good questions, and I had good answers for them.

She was single, but she needed a two-bedroom apartment for when her grandkids spent the night.

After the meeting, I started checking her application. Current address? Checked out. Past address? Checked out. Current employer? Checked out. Three personal references?

Well, you get the idea. Everything was accurate and complete.

When I met with her to finalize the rental, she had her son and his girlfriend with her. I figured they were there to help her move in.

She was so excited about renting such a large apartment (1700 square feet) that she gave them the grand tour. Once she finished, she signed the lease, I collected the deposit and rent, and I gave her the keys.

Next month, rent was on time. Utilities had been moved into her name. Everything was great.

One issue with the apartment was that the off-street parking only held four vehicles, one for each apartment. When I started getting calls from other tenants about them being blocked in or having to maneuver around other cars to get in and out of the driveway, I discovered Linda's visitors were the cause.

I called Linda and explained the problem. "I'll make sure my visitors know where to park," she assured me.

Excellent. One problem solved.

Next month, prompt rent. No more complaints about the parking situation. Everything was good.

Then came month three...

I received a call from the downstairs tenant. There was a small drip in the closet. This meant that either the toilet or the bathtub above the closet was leaking. That was Linda's apartment.

I called Linda to set up a time to look at her bathroom. After work she returned my call. "I won't be home until this weekend," she said, "but my son's staying with me at the moment. He should be able to help."

"Can I have his number?"

"Sure."

I called up her son and he invited me in to check things over.

I fixed the small leak in the bathtub drain. While I was there, I also looked over the sprayer on the kitchen sink and checked the smoke detector. But that's not all I checked....

Every time I visit a tenant to make repairs, I make a surreptitious scan of the apartment.

- I check the cleanliness of the unit.

- I smell for any strange odors that might indicate drug use.

- I see the refrigerator is working and look inside.

- I check the condition of the carpets and walls.

- I make sure the tenant is taking out the trash.

- I check for signs of pets, such a pet toys or a litter box.

During this visit, I noticed the single queen-sized bed. The back bedroom just had boxes in it, no furniture or sleeping area for those grandkids Linda expected

I decided to dig deeper. One of the other tenants was a friend, who had been renting for nearly nine years. "Hey, can you let me know when you see Linda coming and going?" I asked.

"Who's Linda?" he asked.

This surprised me. "She's been renting the upstairs apartment for three months. Her son's staying there while she's gone this weekend."

He laughed. "I've only seen this son and his girlfriend. I haven't seen a Linda." I had no reason to disbelieve him.

When I got home, I called Linda. "I just wanted to let you know the problem's been fixed," I said.

"That's good."

I wanted to probe a bit. "How do you enjoy all this sunny weather we've been having?"

"Oh, it's been great. I love going to the park with my grandkids."

"Did you go down Saturday? It was beautiful."

"We spent most of the afternoon there, playing. He loves the swings."

What she didn't know, obviously, is that it had been wet most of the week. On Saturday, it had poured all day.

I confronted her about it. "Linda, I know you're not living in the apartment. None of the neighbors have seen you since you signed the lease. And the weather was horrible on Saturday."

"I can't believe you're saying that. The neighbors are wrong. And I got my Saturdays confused, that's all. It's been a long week."

"Okay, forget it. How about on this Saturday I'll stop by and show you the repairs I made."

"That'll be fine."

On Friday, Linda called. "I have to go out of town this weekend. It's last-minute, I know. How about you stop by one night this coming week?"

"How about Tuesday?" I said.

"That'll work. Tuesday it is."

And then, on Monday, another phone call. "Look, I'm so sorry, but I'll be out of town again. How about this weekend?"

"Saturday afternoon?"

"Yeah, Saturday afternoon's perfect."

On Saturday, I knocked on the apartment door. The girlfriend answered.

"Is Linda here?"

"Linda? She moved to Florida three months ago."

"This is her apartment."

"Oh, she gave us this apartment when she moved."

I now knew definitively I had two tenants living in my apartment who did not sign a lease. All the utilities were in Linda's name, not in her son's name or in this girlfriend's name.

If it looks like a duck and swims like a duck and quacks like a duck, it's a duck.

These two looked like squatters and acted like squatters—they were squatters.

So I informed them of the situation. "The lease is between myself and Linda. You and your boyfriend aren't allowed to live here."

That's when a guy comes to the door, and it's not the son. And he's big. "Go away. This is none of your business."

Did I mention he was big? And I was alone, so I left. I went directly to the police station. "Do you have an officer available to accompany me?" I explained the situation.

Back at the apartment, I knocked. The big guy answered. "I thought I told you to go away."

"You're trespassing on private property," I told him. "You and the girl need to leave."

The big guy turned to the officer. "He can't kick us out."

"He can. He has every right to say who can and can't be on his property."

"And I don't want them on my property," I said.

This is when they got really mad and said they were going to get Linda's son, since it was mostly his stuff in the apartment. They stormed out of the building and got in their car.

This officer knew what he was doing. "Can I see your license and registration, please?" he asked.

Neither of them had a valid license.

"Please get out of the car, then."

They obeyed and walked, instead of drove, to the son's workplace. It turns out he didn't have a valid license either, and so all three returned to the apartment on foot.

This took them five hours, round trip.

Meanwhile, I called a couple buddies to help me remove all the belongings from the apartment. Four hours later, we had everything in black plastic garbage bags in the parking area, next to their car. We removed the furniture and put it by the car as well, with a tarp over top, just in case it rained.

When they returned, the apartment was emptied and the locks changed. They were livid.

"You have 24 hours to remove your belongings before I haul them to the dump," I told them. "And I don't want to see you anywhere on this property except right here, in the parking area."

After a good evening's work, I went home. To my surprise, when I drove by the next morning, everything was gone. I don't know where they went. I never heard from them again.

Now I just had to deal with Linda.

I called. No answer. I called again. No answer. For a week, no answer. Meanwhile, I was preparing the apartment to rent again.

The next week, I received notice that Linda had taken her name off the utilities. Apparently, she had learned what had happened.

Since her lease was for a year, she was still obligated for another eight months of rent. But since she lived in Florida and wouldn't be back in the apartment, I decided to re-rent it as quickly as possible and forget about taking her to small claims.

Lesson learned: Even if you think you've found a great tenant, be sure to check in every once in a while.

Surprisingly, this is not an isolated incident. Many people cannot rent an apartment on their own, so they have a relative rent the apartment for them. Over the past 20 years, I have had this happen to me four times. Each time, it took me three to four months to figure it out.

16 - The Closed Door

In March 2003, Bill and Jane moved in. I didn't hear from them much, except for the occasional call about something needing repaired.

Every time I stopped by for general maintenance, however, it was the same thing.

Knock, Knock.

A voice through the door: "Who is it?"

"Your landlord."

"Just a minute."

The minute, without fail, became two minutes, then three, sometimes four and five.

Then the door would open. "Come on in."

Even if you're not a landlord, your Spidey-sense is probably tingling by now. Obviously, something was going on—and they did not want me to see.

It was something big, I found out later. In September, to be exact.

I received a phone call from a police officer in the county in which Bill and Jane's apartment was located.

"Could you tell me about the layout of the apartment?" he asked.

I knew this officer, so I felt comfortable answering his questions.

I detailed the apartment. It had a front and side door, with two bedrooms in the back. The front door entered the living room, which led to the dining room. Next to that was the kitchen.

The kitchen led to the side door as well as down into the basement, which had multiple rooms.

"There's also a shared garage," I said. "The tenant has access to the leftmost stall."

"How about locks?" he asked. "What kind of locks are on the doors?"

"If you need a key, I can provide you with one," I offered.

"That won't be necessary at the moment. Thank you for your cooperation."

He hung up.

It doesn't take a genius to connect my tenants' secretive manner and the officer's questions. Of course, I could only speculate at the time. As you are at the moment.

It didn't take me long to discover the truth. One of the tenants' neighbors called that evening, and I pieced together the facts of what went down that day.

The short version: Drugs.

The long version: Drug-sniffing dogs discovered a shipment of illegal drugs at the consolidation centers of one of the major package delivery services. The FBI was brought in. The FBI contacted the State Police. The State Police contacted the County Police. The County Police contacted, you guessed it, the City Police.

And where was the package heading? To Bill and Jane.

The County Police had a drug enforcement division with undercover officers, so the police units involved decided to set up a sting operation.

Exiting an unmarked van, the undercover officer delivered the package. My tenants took delivery. The door closed.

All hell broke loose.

Nine police vehicles blasted into the drive, blocked the street, and careened onto the front and side yards to cover both entrances to the property.

Then the County Police kicked in the front door—although I had offered to give them a key.

In quick order, everyone on the property was handcuffed and settled on the couch until a search of the premises had been completed.

The City Canine unit sniffed out the apartment, basement, and garage. They found two mid-size clear, compartmentalized plastic containers. There were 16 compartments, about 200 pills per compartment—approximately 3200 pills.

The sting happened around 3:30 pm, but I didn't hear about it until two hours later. I immediately drove over to see if I could help with anything. Besides providing a key. Obviously, they didn't need one.

When I arrived, officers were loading four people into their vehicles, Jane among them. As a final act of defiance, she left a long, clear mark on a police cruiser with her key as she passed.

Jane's daughter stood on the front yard, watching. I approached her.

"You'll need to pack up your mother's belongings and take them with you. Otherwise, I'll just have to dump them."

She called a friend, packed up the things she wanted, and left.

It was nearly 7 pm, now, but I had to replace the door (which could have been unlocked instead of kicked in), change the locks, and post a notice that the tenants were not allowed on the property. I informed the local police of the notice as well.

It may have been the end of the line for the criminals and police, but the next day I was just starting. Since I didn't know what drugs had been used in the apartment, I decided to do the works: I replaced all the carpet, repainted the entire apartment, and scrubbed everything down, from top to bottom. Oh, and I replaced the front door.

Total bill—$3000. And no way to recover the money. My tenants were receiving free room and board at the county lock-up and I was out three grand.

Later, I discovered that other landlords had similar experiences with my tenants and drugs. Misery loves company, I guess.

If I had known beforehand, I wouldn't have had to rely strictly on my Spidey-sense. And a multi-department sting operation.

17 - When a Tenant Goes on "Holiday"

Sooner or later, it's going to happen. You have a good tenant. Something happens. They go to jail.

Now what?

First, a little background. This applies specifically to Indiana but may be similar to situations in other states. Be sure to be informed on your own state's laws.

Indiana has rental law that addresses the incarceration of a tenant. A landlord can use this to his advantage. One thing it states is that when a tenant is incarcerated, the landlord is allowed to secure the property by changing the locks.

This comes in handy when the incarcerated tenant is behind on rent. You are still legally required to file in small claims court for immediate possession of the unit. When I do this, I explain in a note on the court documents that the tenant is incarcerated. The tenant is then served in jail by the sheriff, and everything's good to go.

Law also requires you to hold the tenant's possessions for 21 days to allow the family time to claim them. If I know the tenant is going to be gone for an extended period, I clean up the apartment, put his possessions in plastic bags, and keep them in a storage unit until the prescribed time has passed. If they aren't claimed by then, I dispose of them.

Remember, even if the tenant owes you money, you cannot keep his belongings from him. In my early days as a landlord, I was scolded for using possessions as ransom. In any case, the possessions aren't normally worth keeping anyway.

I have also had good tenants fall into bad times. If the tenant is up-to-date on payments, I usually wait until rent's due before taking possession.

During this time, the family usually contacts me to see what is happening with the property. This is when I try to find out what my tenant's situation is. I have seen tenants released after only a weekend on "holiday," as I refer to the incarceration. If so, he's back in the property with nothing lost.

The worst situation, though, is when a tenant is incarcerated and you discover later that friends have moved into his unit without your knowledge.

Since the tenant's name is the only one on the lease, you have to tell all these "friends," that they cannot stay in the apartment and that you are changing the locks.

Ninety-nine percent of the time, the friends know what is going on. This isn't the first time they've been involved in this sort of situation.

The other one percent of the time, the friends want to argue and fight. This is easy to deal with. Lease in hand, I call 911.

"Yes, I'm a landlord and I have some trespassers on my property. They refuse to leave. I feel threatened. Will you send an officer to help?"

I've had one officer arrive. I've had six squad cars pull up. It depends on how busy the police are when I call.

After I calmly explain the situation, I sit back and watch the officer detail to the friends how they have no right to be on the property. "Gather your belongings and get moving." Some seasoned officers add, "If you come back, you'll go to jail for trespassing."

Unfortunately, some younger, non-experienced officers don't know rental law. They look lost and call in for help. If this happens, remain calm, explain the situation to the police, and let the trespassers start arguing with the officer. This irritates the officer and makes it easier for you.

One particular experience - Wally and Denise

Here's one example of what happens when a tenant goes to jail.

Wally and Denise were both hardworking tenants, but one morning I received a call that Wally had been arrested for domestic violence for striking Denise.

Denise was the jealous type. Apparently, the argument started while Wally was talking to another woman. Denise pushed Wally; Wally slapped Denise. Crying, Denise took off in Wally's car and called the police. Wally, not knowing that Denise had called the police, called them himself to report that his car had been stolen.

So, when the police arrived, Wally thought they were there because of the stolen car. He started to explain what had happened--including the altercation.

After his story, the police explained how things stood.

"Sir, Denise called to report domestic abuse. Since you've admitted to hitting her, we'll have to take you in."

I found out later that Wally had two previous charges of domestic violence. This third one meant a long "holiday" for him.

Afterward, Denise called so she could get her stuff out of the apartment.

"Your name's not on the lease," I told her. "You'll have to wait until the possession hearing. You'll need Wally's permission to get your stuff, as well."

This required jumping through a number of hoops. She had to create a list of the items she wanted to retrieve from the apartment and get Wally's okay.

Next, I received a call from Wally's mother, who wanted to remove *his* belongings from the apartment. I told her the same thing, that she needed a letter from Wally indicating she had his permission to remove his items from the apartment.

I set up a date and time when they could both meet me at the apartment to clear it out. Anything left behind would be disposed of and included on the cleaning charges applied toward Wally's deposit.

At the damage hearing, no one showed up, so I received a default judgment for the damage amount. I was unable to find Wally once he was released from jail.

I am using Real Tenant History's Tenant APB process to locate Wally, but at this time his location is still unknown.

18 - The Sleeping Boyfriend

Back in 2002, I had a nice single girl rent the upstairs apartment of an old house that had been converted to a duplex. I'll call her Mary.

After about nine months, I received a call from the downstairs tenant. One of the electrical outlets had quit working. I got the message after work and headed over to the apartment. It was about 6 pm.

Now, in this duplex, the electric and gas were separated, but not the water and sewer. This separation of utilities had been done prior to my purchase of the property.

After some basic troubleshooting, I discovered the malfunctioning outlet was on the breaker box for the upstairs apartment.

But why was this an issue now? I asked myself. I'd never had trouble with the upstairs electrical before.

I checked the meter. It had been red-tagged, meaning the electricity had been shut off due to failure to pay.

Mary worked second shift. Since she wasn't home, I tried to call her. No one answered. I knocked on the door, just in case, but no one answered there, either.

As chance would have it, a sheriff deputy showed up at the apartment just then. I was at the meter when I heard him knock on the front door, then ring the door bell.

I walked back up front. "Is there something I can help you with?" I asked.

"I'm here to serve notice for a resident of this apartment. There's a court case scheduled to deal with late child support."

I knew Mary didn't have children. That meant someone was staying with her. "Who are you trying to serve?"

He told me a man's name I didn't know.

As we stood there, we heard movement inside. While we knocked again at the front door, two people I didn't recognize ran out the side door and down the alley.

"I don't know this person you're trying to serve, " I told the officer, "even though I own this apartment. Can I help you out? I'm curious."

"Sure."

I had a key to the apartment, so I unlocked the door. "Would you mind checking it out?" I asked. It was dark, with the power off, and I didn't know who might be inside.

The officer agreed. He went upstairs, spent about a minute inside, then came out and called in additional officers.

"What's going on?" I asked.

"There's a male upstairs, asleep on the couch. On the table in front of him is drug paraphernalia and a bunch of cash. And his pants and underwear are down around his ankles. That's what's going on."

Since he was a county officer, he had called in the local city police and a K9 unit to search the property.

With the power out, the officers performed their search with flashlights. For two hours they scoured the apartment and rounded up drugs, collecting it on the table where the cash was.

This whole time, this strange man slept on the couch, pants around his ankles—completely out.

After they completed the search, the officers decided to wake the man up and question him.

When they woke him, I happened to be trying to catch a parakeet that was flying around the apartment. I didn't want it flying out the door and leave me responsible for losing the tenant's pet, so I heard what followed.

The officers' first question to the man was simple: "Could you please pull up your pants?"

The man complied.

"Who are you?"

He answered with his name.

"Are these drugs and cash yours?"

No, the drugs were not his, and the more than $5000 cash was not his either.

"Who was in the apartment with you? We saw two people leaving."

He had no idea who the people were.

The questioning lasted about an hour. I expected my tenant home soon from second shift.

At 10:30 pm, the tenant arrived. Four police cars were still parked in the street in front of the apartment.

I was sitting on the front porch, awaiting her arrival. I could tell Mary was more than a little concerned by all the activity. She walked up to me. "What's going on?"

"That's a long story. It started because I was looking into why the power in your apartment had been turned off."

"I gave my boyfriend the money. He was supposed to pay the bill."

I told her the rest of the story. Afterward, I said, "You should probably go talk to the police."

Fifteen minutes later, she came back, sat down on the porch, and started to cry.

I told her there were two things that needed to happen if she wanted to continue to rent the apartment. First, she needed to get the electricity turned on first thing in the morning. Second, her boyfriend could no longer be allowed on the property.

She agreed, and I'm happy to say everything was fine between us until she moved.

I have specific wording in the lease indicating the number of occupants allowed in a unit, but without checking in continually, you never know what kind of character a tenant may allow to move in.

In this case, the boyfriend was the tenant predator. He moved from girlfriend to girlfriend, leeching off them.

Since I had his name, I documented it at Real Tenant History, just in case he tries to rent from another area landlord. They'll be able to see his connection to drugs and drug paraphernalia.

That way, no one else has to be caught with his pants down.

19 - What Goes Around ...

You know what karma is, right? In a nutshell, karma is the belief that when you do something good, something good will happen to you. Or, in common speech, "What goes around, comes around."

About 12 years ago, I had a tenant tell me exactly that—"What goes around, comes around." He was right, too, but not in the way he meant it.

This tenant lived in a one-bedroom upstairs apartment. It was a nice little place, and she was a good tenant.

Until her boyfriend moved in.

Things started changing fast then. Let's see...

First, her rent was late.

Next, I received calls that shady-looking people were hanging around the apartment.

Then--domestic abuse.

And finally, the police started showing up at the unit on a regular basis.

Things had gone downhill fast. I'd had enough of the disruptions, and the other tenants on the property were tired of complaining. I laid down the law.

"Your boyfriend is no longer allowed on this property," I told her.

"You can't tell me who can and can't stay with me."

I repeated that I didn't want to see her boyfriend on the property again and left.

Well, I discovered she hadn't bothered to mention the ultimatum to her boyfriend, so the next time I was in the area I stopped by and told him myself.

He said some rather rude things, but it came down to this: "I'm staying."

Now, from what I had heard about the people coming and going from the unit while my tenant was gone, I suspected drug dealing and/or drug use at the property. I decided to exercise the drug policy and default section of the lease.

Criminal/Drug Policy:

1. DRUG-RELATED CRIMINAL ACTIVITY, ON OR NEAR THE SAID PREMISES. Drug-related criminal activity means the illegal manufacture, sale, distribution, use, or possession with intent to manufacture, sell, distribute, or use a controlled substance (as defined in Section 102 of the controlled Substance Act 21 U.S.C. 802)
2. ENGAGE IN ANY ACT INTENDED TO FACILITATE CRIMINAL ACTIVITY, including drug-related criminal activity, on, or near said premises.
3. PERMITTING THE DWELLING UNIT TO BE USED FOR, OR TO FACILITATE CRIMINAL ACTIVITY, including drug-related criminal activity, regardless of whether the individual engaging in such activity is a member of the household or a guest.
4. UNLAWFUL MANUFACTURING, SELLING, USING, STORING, OR KEEPING OR GIVING OF A CONTROLLED SUBSTANCE as defined in I.C. 35-489, at any location, whether on or near the dwelling unit or otherwise.

Defaults Section of Lease:

DEFAULTS. Tenant shall be in default of this Lease if Tenant fails to fulfill any lease obligation or term by which Tenant is bound....

And so on.

In summary, his presence and activity violated the lease, and I just needed to serve notice to end it.

I decided to give my tenant a seven-day "Notice to Quit," one of the many forms available from Real Tenant History. This gave her a week to vacate the property.

When I stopped to deliver the notice, her boyfriend was home. I handed it to him, and he signed for it.

"We've nowhere to move," he said.

"Unfortunately, you violated the lease. It's not my problem."

"What goes around, comes around, buddy. Karma, you know."

"This isn't karma. I'm just following proper procedure, since drugs are suspected of being on the property." He obviously had no idea what was in the lease, since he hadn't been around when it was signed.

I stopped by the apartment after the seven days were up. They were gone. It was later I discovered that what goes around really does come around.

In my city, there is an apartment community that used to be a nursing home. It's not a nice place to rent, since when you rent an "apartment," you have a shared common area, shared bathrooms, and shared kitchen.

Some time after this I found out the boyfriend had become the manger of this facility. Drugs are rampant in the place and the police are there nearly every day.

More to the point, rent is weekly, and if you don't pay, you have 24 hours to vacate the premises. A rule the boyfriend enforces.

And that's karma, folks.

20 - The Eviction Process

It's strange what some tenants will do or say to get themselves evicted.

Once, while working on the basement furnace of a four-unit apartment building, I overheard one tenant, who was behind on his rent, talking to another tenant.

"You know what? Everyone here would be better off if the landlord was gone."

"Gone?"

"Yeah, gone. And, trust me, I'm just the person to make that happen."

This disturbed me more than a little. When I finished my work, I headed to the court house and filed a restraining order against the tenant for threatening my life. He was forced to vacate the premises.

This is not a common reason for eviction, but it happened to me.

It doesn't matter how many rental units you own or how diligently you screen your tenants or whether you have the luck of the Irish—if you're a landlord, sooner or later, you will go through the eviction process. It's imperative you know the process in your city and county for evicting an unwanted tenant.

The primary reason for evicting a tenant is for not paying rent. Other reasons include maintaining a common nuisance, disturbing the peace, or immoral conduct. Whatever the reason, as long as you present it properly in court, you will most likely be granted the eviction.

If you don't do your homework, however, you could lose the case.

The process I'm about to describe comes from more than 25 years of experience of being an independent rental owner, or landlord, in Indiana. In most places, the process will be similar, but be sure to do your research.

The Lease

First, you want to make sure your lease clearly outlines what you, as a landlord, are allowed to do. Here's how mine is worded:

DEFAULTS. Tenant shall be in default of this Lease if Tenant fails to fulfill any lease obligation or term by which Tenant is bound. Subject to any governing provisions of law to the contrary, if Tenant fails to cure any financial obligation within 7 days (or any other obligation within 7 days) after written notice of such default is provided by Landlord to Tenant, Landlord may take possession of the Premises without further notice (to the extent permitted by law), and without prejudicing Landlord's rights to damages. In the alternative, Landlord may elect to cure any default and the cost of such action shall be added to Tenant's financial obligations under this Lease. Tenant shall pay all costs, damages, and expenses (including reasonable attorney fees and expenses) suffered by Landlord by reason of Tenant's defaults. All sums of money or charges required to be paid by Tenant under this Lease shall be additional rent, whether or not such sums or charges are designated as "additional rent". The rights provided by this paragraph are cumulative in nature and are in addition to any other rights afforded by law.

This paragraph ensures that the tenant agrees to these rights when he signs the lease. It does not preclude you from obtaining an eviction notice, but it's great documentation when you need to request one.

The Possession Hearing

All evictions begin with a possession hearing. This is when the landlord presents his case as to why the tenant should be removed from the rental unit. To start the ball rolling, you have to file for a possession hearing date at the local courthouse.

Once the paperwork for the possession hearing is filed, the papers must be served to the tenant in question. This can be done three ways -- through certified mail, sheriff, or private process server. Each option has its downside.

Certified mail only works if the tenant actually accepts the letter. They are not required to accept it. The Post Office will hold the unaccepted letter for up to 10 days before returning it to the court house, and the court will process it as undeliverable. This means that the tenant was never served and you have to start the process all over again.

Using a sheriff to serve the notice has its own problems. Sheriff Departments are busy. They will serve the notice as time allows. I've found it takes one to two weeks for notices to get served by the sheriff.

The quickest way to serve a notice is to use a private process server, which will get the job done in 24 hours. However, this is also the most expensive way to serve a notice.

I have been using a private process server since I discovered the hard way the sheriff's office serves notices as they have time. My experience, in a nutshell, was this:

I showed up for a possession hearing.

"I'm sorry. The sheriff's department was busy with holiday vacations. It couldn't get around to serving your non-paying tenant. Please reschedule for two weeks from now and hope they get served the notice by then. Thank you!"

Needless to say, I was not amused.

In any case, let's assume the notice is served. Most courthouses have one day a week set aside for eviction hearings.

In my case, it's Friday starting at 8:30 am. In Allen County, Indiana, there's a 20-minute grace period before the tenant is deemed a no-show. In Noble County, Indiana, the grace period is 15 minutes. It varies from county to county and state to state.

In my experience, 95% of tenants will not show up at the hearing, which means you win a "default possession" for the rental unit. The evicted tenant now has seven days to vacate the premises.

Eviction

If the tenant does not vacate the premises within seven days, it's back to the court house to sign the "rite book." This may be called something else in your county.

The rite alerts the sheriff's department that the tenant refuses to vacate the premise and that you will require their assistance. The sheriff department receives the rite from the court house within 5 days and puts the visit on its schedule.

In Allen County, this can take one to four weeks, depending on the department's schedule.

The sheriff will call the day before he's ready to visit the tenant. You need to make yourself available to secure the property.

Normally when I receive this call, I also call the tenant to let him know the sheriff and I will be at the unit the next day to remove him from the property. I am not required to do this, but I do it anyway.

Many times, the tenant responds with some version of "I can't move out that quickly." Never mind the process thus far has taken up to two months. The tenant still feels as though he has been treated unfairly, even though he has been living rent free during the entire eviction process.

The next day, I arrive a little early and wait for the sheriff. When he arrives, he usually takes charge.

He knocks on the rental unit's door. When the tenant opens it, he asks, "Do you know why I'm here?"

They usually say, "Yes."

"You have 20 minutes to remove your belongings and vacate the premises. Anything you can't take now, you have seven days to contact the landlord and get."

I usually give the tenant a four-hour window to collect his belongings during that seven-day period. After the week's over, I dispose of anything left behind.

During this seven-day period, landlords are allowed to charge a storage fee equal to what a storage facility would charge, and the tenant cannot collect his belongings without paying the storage fee.

After this, you enter the next phase of the process.

The Damage Hearing

The damage hearing is usually 30-45 days after the possession hearing. This is when you present and explain to the court what the damages were, including any back rent, unpaid utilities, and late fees the evicted tenant owes.

It is the landlord's responsibility to prove all damages, past due rent, and late fees. That is why it is vital to document the lease and its provisions. Indiana law indicates that a lease *is* enforceable, whether written or verbal.

The damage hearing is similar to those daytime court shows on TV. The atmosphere is usually relaxed. The judge will explain why you and the tenant are there, and each side has an opportunity to tell his story.

Now, remember, a story is just a story unless you have documentation and pictures to back it up.

I think the most important item you need during the damage hearing is the original written and signed lease. This proves what your tenant agreed to when they moved in.

Other important items include: move-in and move-out pictures, receipts for all repairs and materials, and documentation for all written and verbal communication with the tenant during their tenancy.

This means you need to keep copies of notes, letters, and other forms of written communication the tenant has provided during his time in your unit.

Using the tools provided by Real Tenant History, I am able to easily document these things over time. If the need arises to take a tenant to small claims for a damage hearing, I can generate all the necessary paperwork directly from the website. This is a huge time-saver.

If the tenant fails to show up for the damage hearing, you receive what is known as a summary judgment. This means you receive a judgment for exactly what you were asking from the courts.

Over the past 20+ years, I have had probably 40+ damage hearings. With proper documentation and preparation, I have never lost a single claim.

If you win the case, that's when the real work begins—collecting your money.

For details on debt collections, see Appendix 2, which deals with small claims limits and collection of debts.

Lessons Learned

If you remember one thing from this chapter, remember this:

Document Everything!

One more time, in unison—**Document Everything!**

Keep track of everything you can regarding a tenant. Hopefully, you'll never need it, but at some point, you might. If you're using the tools provided by Real Tenant History, you'll be able to keep track of the information with minimal effort, and when you need it, the site can create all the reports necessary for filing a claim.

Finally, let's look at the time involved in removing an unwanted tenant:

- Preparing paperwork for eviction – 2 hours

- Spending time at the court house – 1-3 hours

- Waiting to have paperwork served – 14 days

- Waiting to vacate premises – 7 days

- Waiting for the sheriff to schedule a vacate premises visit – up to 4 weeks

- Waiting for tenant to pick up remaining belongings – 7 days

- Waiting for damage hearing – 45 days

- Collecting the debt – Unlimited

Wouldn't it be better to avoid renting to such a tenant in the first place? With access to landlord reviews and ratings, you might avoid the entire situation. That's what Real Tenant History is all about, helping you minimize the 20% of tenants that consume 80% of your time and energy.

21 - Fifty Trash Bags

Ring-Ring!

I answered the phone. One of my tenants was on the other end.

"We'll be moving out at the end of the month."

Tenants sometimes call to tell me they'll be moving, but there's a specific procedure for such a notification. I tried to explain the process outlined in the lease: "You'll need to send a written notice in the mail to the proper PO box. Also, you're required to give at least 30 days notice. The details are in your lease."

"Okay. I understand. Thanks."

That was the end of the conversation. It was the 17th of the month.

And so the story begins....

I never received a letter. The tenant's lease was set to auto-renew for a three-month period if I didn't receive the 30-day notification.

I didn't. The lease renewed.

When the first of the month came around, I went to the Post Office to collect rent. The tenant hadn't sent any.

I sent out a late notice.

The following Monday, I returned to the Post Office. Still nothing.

I decided to visit the apartment to talk with the tenant. It was locked. No one appeared to be home. I entered and found this:

This is the kitchen, full of boxes and a computer chair, with a computer monitor sitting in it.

This is the dining area, with a vacuum cleaner, more boxes, and furniture.

The freezer: still full of items, mostly unopened and perfectly good.

And here's the master bedroom, with piles and piles of stuff, including all the "new baby" items from a recent addition to the family.

And the upstairs bedroom, complete with vanity mirror, dresser, and yet more boxes. Some of the boxes were full, others empty.

I couldn't tell if the tenant had moved or not. I didn't find any beds, so I assumed they were in the process of moving,

I called the tenant on his cell phone. It went to voice mail. I left this message:

"Hello, this is your landlord. I stopped by the apartment today to check on you. It appears you are in the process of moving. Please give me a call."

No return call that day. Or the next. Or the next. I decided to call again.

"Hello," I told the voice mail, "this is your landlord. I called a few days ago, but I haven't had a return call yet. You are now 10 days past your move-out date. I will be placing all your belongings in trash bags and putting them in the back parking area. If you wish to retrieve them, you have until the end of the week. After that, I'm taking them to the dump."

Thirty minutes later, I received a call. Seems my message worked.

"We'd prefer if you wouldn't leave our stuff outside. If you'd just pack it up and leave it in the apartment, we'll come get it."

"I've already changed the door locks and deadbolts," I told him. "You won't be able to get in the apartment. Here's what I'll do. I'll put your stuff out back Friday morning. You have until noon to pick it up. At one, my cleaning crew will take whatever's left to the dump."

So, Friday morning we hauled more than fifty 55-gallon trash bags out of the apartment and into the back parking area. It was at least four loads for a regular pick-up truck.

The tenants arrived at 8:00 am. They ripped open every bag, scavenged through each one, took what they wanted, and left the rest.

Come 1:00 pm, my cleaning crew had to clean up a *second* time. They gathered the debris strewn across the parking area into new trash bags and headed for the dump.

Here's the "Termination of Tenancy Report" I created with Real Tenant History that takes into account the time and effort spent twice moving tenants who didn't make the effort to send a written notice:

Security Deposit Notice to Tenant - Termination of Tenancy

Forwarding Address:

Past Tenant	Attainment, Inc.
Address Blocked	P.O. Box 563
Kendallville, IN 46755	Kendallville, IN 46755
	(260) 347-5835

Sent September 5th, 2012

You must respond to this notice by mail within 7 days after receipt of same, otherwise you will forfeit the amount claimed for damages.

On or about _ September 1st 1st, 2013_____, your occupancy of the premises commomly kn
_ 123 1/2 N Orchard_, Kendallville, IN 46755 terminated pursuant to statute,
this notice is given to advise you of the items charged against your security deposit
as follows:

(A) Rent Deposit $550.00
(B) Pet Deposit $_____ Less $_____ (Non Refundable)
(C) Key Deposit $0
(D)   Net Deposit Refundable .... ($550.00)

Tenant Moved without notifying Landlord after 7 days

CHARGES AGAINST SECURITY DEPOSIT   Cost to Repair/Replace
1. Clean Toilet (1 Hour @ 25.00 per hour) $ 25.00
2. Replace 6 Blinds Material Plus Labor (5.24*6) + 50.00 $ 81.44
3. Clean Stove (1 Hours) $ 25.00
4. Carpet Cleaning $ 192.54
5. Empty and Clean Fridge $ 125.00
6. Pick up Trash (Pictures Available) - 6 Hours $ 150.00
7. Three Load to Dump @ 75.00 per load) $ 225.00
8. Unpaid Gas Utility (Paid by Landlord) $ 248.00
9.

(E) Total Damages $1,071.98
(F) Unpaid Rent   July, August, September 2013 .... $ 1,650.00
               *Rent Through end of Lease
(G) Other Charges
      Court Charges $92.00   1 Person
      Late Fees $ 225.00
      Late Fees $ -

      Other $_____ Explain _____ $317.00
(H) Total Charges against security deposit   (E) plus (F) plus (G) $3,038.98

(I) Refund of Rent From _____ to _____ @ $____ per day $0.00

BALANCE   (D) minus (H) Plus (I)   ($2,488.98)
If Positive Balance Due You *** Check Enclosed ***
If Negative-Amount Due us *** **Please pay within 7 days** *** If Payment not received within 7 days, this
Matter will be turned over to our Attorney.
Remit Payment to :   **Attainment, Inc.**
                     P.O. Box 563
                     Kendallville, IN 46755
                     (260) 347-5835

Date: _____   Signed by: _____

This incident taught me several lessons:

First, if a tenant gives notice, take them at his word. Notice is notice. You have no obligation to take care of their property after the official move-out date.

Second, if you don't receive written notice, but you do record the verbal notice, save it. Most voice mail services allow you to save a message locally, which you can submit during a small claim hearing.

Third, don't let a tenant "take his time" moving. Pack up their stuff and either donate it to Goodwill or send it to the dump.

Your time and talents cost money. Unless you are willing to spend them on a tenant who has abused his end of the deal, you have no obligation to go above and beyond your duty as a landlord.

A tenant can try to take his time moving, but you don't have to let him take *your* time doing it.

22 - Spotless

When someone moves into an apartment or house, I have a few documents we review together. I take the time to read through the entire lease with them, just to be sure they understand. I also go through the Move-Out Checklist.

The new tenants initial each page of the lease, sign the last page, and sign and date the Move-Out Checklist.

I do this so there is no confusion concerning the expectations of how the rented space should look when they move out.

In a nutshell, the Move-Out Checklist is broken into three sections.

- What I expect them to clean when they move out.

- What I will charge them if they choose not to clean

- What painting costs are for more than normal wear-and-tear damage to walls.

The form looks like this:

We would like to ensure that your security deposit is returned after you move. Please follow the guidelines below and we will cheerfully and promptly refund your deposit.

- *Follow your lease requirements.*
- *Empty and clean the stove, refrigerator, other appliances, closets and cupboards.*
- *Clean out all storage areas.*
- *Leave floors, walls, woodwork, and ceilings in good condition.*
- *Sweep and mop all vinyl floors and ceramic tile.*
- *Vacuum all carpets.*
- *Dispose of all trash.*
- *Clean windows.*
- *Replace burned-out light bulbs.*
- *Return keys to apartment management.*

- *Be certain all rent and other charges are paid in full.*
- *Leave a forwarding address.*
- *Contact appropriate utility companies and have utilities put back in the name of Attainment, Inc.*

When guidelines are completed, Attainment, Inc. staff will be happy to schedule a walk-through and inspect the rental unit. Assuming the guidelines above have been met, your security deposit will be returned in 45 days or less. Should any of the following items be missing, damaged, or inoperative, our replacement costs will be charged to you.

- Light Bulbs
- Light Fixtures
- Range Burners and Drip Pans
- Windows and Screens
- Storm Door Items
- Carpet, Tile, Floor Coverings
- Shelves for Refrigerator
- Shelves for Range
- Shelves for Closets
- Sink Stoppers
- Ceiling Fans
- Other Specified Items

If cleaning the apartment is necessary, there will be extra charges deducted from your security deposit. We will provide you with an itemized list of deductions. Any charges not covered after deducting from the security deposit will be billed to your forwarding address. Following is a list of minimum cleaning charges, which could be higher if cleaning takes longer than expected. Please note this list is not all-inclusive; you can be charged for cleaning or repairing not on the list.

Item	Min. Charge	Item	Min. Charge
Wall Washed	$90	Windows Cleaned	$20
Range Cleaned	$35	Cabinets Cleaned	$25
Refrigerator Cleaned	$40	Trash Removed	$50
Floors Swept	$25	Bathtub Cleaned	$30
Bathroom Vanity Cleaned	$20	Toilet Cleaned	$25
Unreturned Keys	$35	Carpet Cleaning	$50 +

Phend's Carpet Cleaning and Upholstery is the only certified Carpet Cleaner for Attainment, Inc. (Please feel free to contact them at ###-###-####.

If painting is required (for more than normal wear-and-tear), we will charge the following:

Studio Apartment	$150
1-Bedroom Unit	$200
2-Bedroom Unit	$250
3-Bedroom Unit	$300
4-Bedroom Unit	$350

Any additional damages to walls, doors, cupboards, etc., will be billed at an hourly rate of $25.00 per hour plus materials.

I have read and understand the move-out check list.

_____   _____

Resident Signature   *Date*

_____   _____

Resident Signature   *Date*

Even though we go through this document in its entirety, you can imagine the condition of some of the rental units when a tenant moves out.

But instead of imagining, let me show you a few examples.

Over the years, I have learned to take eight to ten pictures of the unit when the new tenant moves in. I transfer them to the tenant's account in Real Tenant History. When they move out, I take the same 8-10 pictures and store them in the tenant's account in the Move-Out section. It only takes a few minutes to snap the pictures, but it can save you a tremendous amount of money if you need to take the tenant to small claims court.

The following examples are from tenants who indicated they left the apartment "spotless" and were charged for the clean-up of their so-called spotless apartment.

I ended up taking these tenants to small claims court due to the amount of cleanup needed.

The tenant who left the above disaster contested the clean-up charges in small claims because he left the apartment "spotless."

As always, my attorney had copies of the Move-Out photos. He happily presented the above picture after the tenant made his "spotless" claim.

We won the full amount for damages.

When these tenants moved out, they swore up and down that they had cleaned the kitchen. When I presented this picture at small claims court, they said, "That is not our apartment!"

I spent several months helping these tenants get caught up with rent. In January 2013, they went through a difficult time, so I set up a payment plan.

Over a six-month period, I heard numerous reasons why they did not have the rent. She lost her job because she needed time off due to childbirth. His hours were cut back due to a slow-down at work. Hospital expenses, etc.

After those six months, I decided I had done everything I could for them. I told them their lease would not be renewed. They came up with $1000, and I agreed to extent the lease for 30 days at a time, as long as they continued to make payments.

That did not happen. They left the above colossal mess.

After all the help and extensions, I expected they would clean up so they could at least receive a portion of their security deposit back.

This tenant moved out and decided to "take his time." This was the fridge, ten days after their move-out date.

These tenants gave proper notice before moving out, moved out on time, but left a bunch of stuff behind. They didn't leave a forwarding address and they wouldn't answer their phone, so I finally decided to gather everything up in trash bags and leave them outside the back door. I hoped they would finally respond to one of my messages and pick up the rest of their belongings.

I left a new message about leaving everything out back. That's when they returned my call.

"Please, we don't want our stuff outside. And why did you change the locks? We're still moving out."

"Your lease is up," I told them. "You gave me notice."

"We're taking our time to move."

"You can't do that. You're not paying rent."

They left the items in the trash bags behind the apartment for nearly a week. When they finally came to pick them up, they ripped them open, took what they wanted, and left the rest—all over the parking lot. I ended up hauling away two truckloads of trash.

I took the tenant to small claims for a number of issues:

- Trash Removal
- Cleaning (Over 20 hours)
- Unpaid Utilities – Water and Gas
- Back Rent
- Late Fees
- Rent for the month when they were "taking their time moving."

This is not what we would call a spotless kitchen.

Somewhere in the picture above is a kitchen sink. It's nearly unrecognizable because the tenant seems to have emptied the contents of the cupboard onto the counter—this on top of a sink full of dirty dishes.

Apparently, it wasn't worth their time to wash the dishes and pack them up.

Every time a tenant does this, it amazes me. First, he will have to buy new dishes. Second, he will get charged for the cleanup. And third, failing to leave the apartment in its proper state affects the TILE (Tenant Information Landlord Evaluation) score on Real Tenant History. Tenants like this will have difficulty finding a place to rent if they continue to leave apartments in this condition.

Since I use Real Tenant History to manage all my properties, applications, and tenants, I also have full access to past landlord experiences with the tenant.

"But we did clean the kitchen!" they protested. Really?

Here's another clean kitchen! Tenants seem to have an issue with cleaning kitchens. The dirtiest place when someone moves out is invariably the kitchen.

What people don't realize is that a dirty kitchen is an expensive kitchen.

- Stove Cleaned $35
- Refrigerator Cleaned $40
- Trash Removed $50
- Floors Swept $25
- Walls Washed $90

Total $240

When tenants rent a house, they are also required to pick up the trash in the yard. This back porch held more than 300 beer cans and 200 beer bottles. It must have been quite a party!

Perhaps this tenant was saving cans to recycle. I'm not sure why he saved them all across the back yard, though.

Since this was a house, the tenant was responsible for the condition of the yard as well as the inside of the house.

Three hundred beer cans, mostly tall boys, is quite the investment. It's unfortunate, then, to realize the tenant moved because he couldn't keep up with rent. That might have been a better investment.

One thing I take into account when renting is whether a tenant will be a good neighbor, since he will be living near other tenants. Leaving garbage sit around is not the trait of a good neighbor.

"But I took out the trash!" Leaving a pile of trash in the backyard does not constitute "taking out" the trash.

At this apartment, we pay for garbage collection and provide a three-yard dumpster. The dumpster is next to the alley, which is next to the rental unit.

I didn't think I was expecting too much when I hoped to see the trash actually put *in* the dumpster. Silly me.

This tenant lived in this apartment for three months, then left without notice, his back rent due.

When I showed this tenant the apartment, he had his "ex-wife" and two "kids" with him. He was on disability, but it was enough to cover rent, utilities, and general needs.

He said he'd be living alone in the apartment.

Two months later, a neighbor contacted me and said there were multiple people living in the apartment with him.

Multiple, in this case, meant seven—friends, a niece, her boyfriend, and two of their friends.

I told him this was not allowed. I had to act quickly; I assumed the others were helping with rent. Once they left, he wouldn't be able to afford rent. Since he was on disability, I couldn't collect a small claim against him, so I didn't want him to incur any additional charges.

He moved. He cleaned nothing and left three truckloads of junk.

I can only assume he is doing the same thing to his new landlord.

When someone moves out, we expect them to take ALL their belongings. This includes all furniture.

The same tenant left all his used furniture, including a couch placed in this unnatural position. I think it was an act of defiance.

All these Move-Out pictures were stored in Real Tenant History along with all Move-Out charges. This makes it convenient to record and report what was and wasn't cleaned every time a tenant moves out. You always hope for a "spotless" apartment, but at least you have proof if it wasn't.

23 - The Maintenance Game

The authors of this book are Independent Rental Owners (IROs), so we tend to look at maintenance and repairs from the standpoint of time, cost, experience, and service.

In larger rental communities, there's usually a maintenance crew that has the resources to handle nearly all the tasks and repairs that arise. But as an IRO, I can either be the maintenance crew *or* I can hire the job out to a local provider.

This is where assessing cost vs. experience comes in. As an IRO, I cannot afford to hire out every job that comes up, so I have to pick and choose what I can do efficiently myself and what an expert can do better and quicker.

Here are some examples of common jobs and the thinking that goes into handling them.

Changing Locks

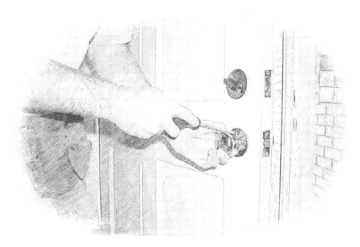

Last week I received a call from a gentleman who had his girlfriend living with him. She was not on the lease. There was an issue between the two and he wanted the locks changed.

The cost would be billed straight to the tenant, so whether I hired the job out or not, I would not be bearing the cost.

I told him I would come over and do the work myself for $45. My cost for lock and deadbolt is $20. The job took about 15 minutes. My minimum bill rate is one hour, and I charge $25 an hour when doing work at an apartment at a tenant's request.

If I would have hired the local locksmith, it would have cost about $100, plus I would have had to pay up front and get reimbursed by the tenant.

So I change locks myself. I also keep old locks and deadbolts so I can use them on a different property in the future.

Kitchen, Bathroom, and Bathtub Faucets

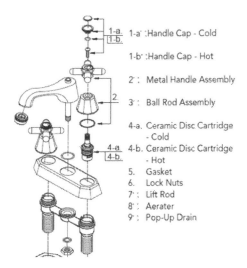

1-a : Handle Cap - Cold

1-b : Handle Cap - Hot

2 : Metal Handle Assembly

3 : Ball Rod Assembly

4-a. Ceramic Disc Cartridge - Cold

4-b. Ceramic Disc Cartridge - Hot

5. Gasket
6. Lock Nuts
7 : Lift Rod
8 : Aerater
9 : Pop-Up Drain

Remember: plumbers are expensive.

A kitchen sink faucet is probably the easiest of the three faucets to repair or replace. If it starts to drip or leaks a little by the handles, it's cost effective to replace it. If it has a sprayer, it's about $50 for a full metal replacement.

Don't go for the least expensive plastic model. It'll just give you headaches down the road.

You can replace a kitchen faucet in about 30 minutes. If a plumber does it, it'll take the same amount of time, but you'll pay about $200 in materials and labor.

A bathroom vanity faucet is a little harder because the space is tighter. Because of this, the costs even out whether you do it yourself or hire a plumber to do it.

Finally, the bathtub faucet. Most bathtub faucets will allow you to replace nearly any part of the fixture. Knowing how a bathtub faucet is built will provide you with every piece of information you need to repair it.

The last thing you want to do is cut open the wall to replace the entire fixture, but if that's required, do it. A little drywall mud, drywall tape, a couple drywall screws, some sanding and painting, and it'll be as good as new.

A full bathtub faucet replacement costs about $150, plus the cost of fixing the wall. So about $250. If you hire a plumber, you'll spend $250 and still have to fix the wall yourself.

Heating and Cooling

These costs vary dramatically, depending on the type of heating and cooling you provide the tenants. For this example, I'm going to assume there is central air-conditioning and gas-forced heat.

If you have a newer furnace, there are a few items you should keep on hand for an easy fix.

Igniter

The furnace igniter is an easy piece to replace on a furnace. Usually, only two screws need removed. As with all electrical appliances, make sure the electricity is turned off prior to replacing the igniter.

If the furnace is not igniting, remove this piece and inspect it. If it's cracked, replace it. It costs between $15 and $30.

Typically, this type of repair is not at the tenant's expense, so saving on labor is like putting money in your pocket. A heating/cooling company will charge about $40 for the ignitor and at least a one-hour service call.

If you do it, it should not take more than five minutes.

Furnace vacuum switch

Again, only two screws need removed. Two hoses and two wires attach to the switch. Make sure you pay attention to which hose goes where and how the wires are attached. Just replace them properly on the new piece and you're good to go.

The switch costs between $30 and $40.

Error Codes

Also, make sure you know what the blinking lights on the control panel mean. There should be a diagram on the inside cover of the furnace that explains them, similar to what follows:

These are some common Trane furnace error codes.

Flashing slow: Normal no call for heat

Flashing fast: Normal call for heat

Continuous on: Replace control

Continuous off: Check for power

2 flashes: System lockout (no flame) or reversed polarity

3 flashes: Pressure switch problem

4 Flashes: Thermal (limit) protection off

5 Flashes: Flame sensed with gas valve off

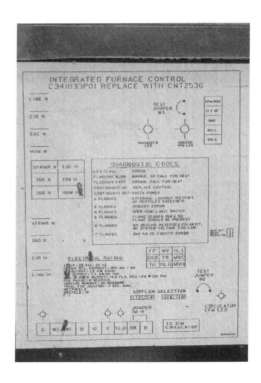

Every furnace manufacturer is different, so become familiar with your particular band.

In a typical year, I perform maintenance on my rentals' heating and cooling systems about 15 times. I end up calling in a professional about 2-3 times. Since a service call costs between $100 and $200, I save between $1200 and $2400 a year doing the rest of the maintenance myself.

Clogged Drains

This item is simple. If you have a clogged sink, toilet, or bathtub, you can usually clean it out yourself.

Don't waste time with "over-the-counter" drain cleaners. They work slowly and, in most cases, not as well as they should.

If you have access to the drain and trap, take the pipes apart and make sure no foreign objects are inside.

If everything is clear, get the plunger. One thing to keep in mind: you are trying to pull the clog toward you, not push it away.

Once you see some draining, get some good drain cleaner and follow the instructions.

Liquid Fire – My Favorite

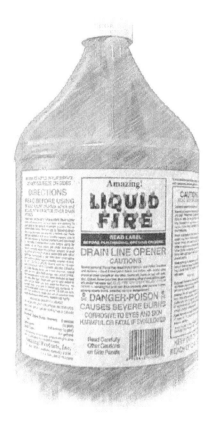

This is the best drain cleaner I've ever used. Remember, follow the instructions exactly. It tends to generate a lot of heat, up to 250 degrees.

Plumbers have been using this for years. It's their little secret. Not every retailer sells it, but most **Do-It Best Stores do**.

I have seen it eat through tree roots near an old clay tile. I once put some in a glass, added a little water, and dropped a penny in. The penny disintegrated in no time.

<u>Be very careful when using Liquid Fire.</u>

When I use it, I try to make sure I run at least 50 gallons of hot water down the drain to clear it out. Then I run another 50 gallons of cold water. This ensures the drain is completely clear and that no Liquid Fire is left.

Other Areas

There are many other area where you can save money by doing the work yourself. But there are also times it makes sense to hire a professional, whether because of difficulty or because of the time required.

Following are a few suggestions:

Task	Hire out work/Do it yourself
New Roofing	Hire a professional
Minor Roofing Repairs	Do it yourself
Concrete work	Hire a professional
Replacing Siding	Do it yourself
Screen Doors	Do it yourself
Replace water line	Hire a professional
Replace Sewer Line	Hire a professional
Fix a broken Window	Do it yourself
Repair Screens	Do it yourself
Replace carpeting	Hire a professional
Carpet cleaning	Hire a professional
Interior Painting	Do it yourself
Minor drywall repair	Do it yourself
Replacing all drywall	Hire a professional

Whenever it is feasible to do the work yourself in a timely, efficient manner, you can save yourself a significant amount of money.

Finally, I use the maintenance feature at Real Tenant History to keep manage of all the maintenance items completed at my properties. This helps me track expenses by property, unit, and tenant.

It also allows me to keep a To-do List of items that are not urgent but I need to address when I have time.

24 - Choices, Choices

In the rental business, there are a lot of choices. Do I rent to this potential tenant? Do I wait another week for rent? Do I let go of the dying hope of ever collecting this debt?

And so on. We've covered most of those.

But there are also questions of how to set up the apartment in the first place, and we're going to examine a few of those choices now.

Carpet or Tile?

Perhaps you've walked into an apartment and noticed that all the floors are either linoleum, tile, or wood laminate. If you're the curious type, you probably wondered, "Why isn't there any carpet?"

The reason is this—carpet is a hassle. I have become more and more frustrated with having to replace the carpet in a unit every one to three years.

Technically, carpet is supposed to last seven years in the rental business. You put it on the books as an asset and depreciate it over those seven years. If a tenant damages the carpet, you only charge them for the *remaining* life of the carpet.

And, then, of course, you have to buy all new carpet.

To avoid these expensive replacements, I decided to replace the flooring in one of my units with something more durable and permanent.

Before the switch, kitchens and bathrooms got the linoleum and everywhere else got carpet. Carpet's more inviting and it's warmer on bare feet. But with the price of carpet nearly doubling over the previous 10 years, and with the price of installation following, it was getting really expensive.

Here's what the typical cost would be:

Rental Size	Square Yards	Carpet Cost	Installation
Efficiency	50 Sq/Yds	$1,120.00	$300.00
1 Bedroom	70 sq/yds	$1,568.00	$300.00
2 Bedroom	80 sq/yds	$1,795.00	$400.00
3 Bedroom	100 sq/yds	$2,241.00	$450.00
4 Bedroom	120 sq/yds	$2,689.00	$525.00

This was a cost I was incurring every one to three years and it took between three and four months of rent for me to recoup my expenses.

Now, with ceramic tile, I have increased the floor life from one to three years to nine to twelve years.

Since I'm at Home Depot or Lowe's once a week, I always check to see if they have bulk ceramic tile on sale. When I find a good deal, I buy it for the next time I'll need it.

I can also put the tile down myself, so I save one installation as well. My flooring costs are much lower, assuming I can get 12"x12" tile for $1 each.

My typical tile costs come out like this:

Rental Size	Square Yards	Carpet Cost	Installation
Efficiency	50 Sq/Yds	$550.00	$0
1 Bedroom	70 sq/yds	$730.00	$0
2 Bedroom	80 sq/yds	$820.00	$0
3 Bedroom	100 sq/yds	$975.00	$0
4 Bedroom	120 sq/yds	$1200.00	$0

That's a lot of savings!

Another advantage is that even when the carpet didn't need replaced when a tenant moved out, I still needed to have it professionally cleaned. That cost between $150 and $400.

Now all I do is scrub and mop the floor myself. Sure, I spend more of my own time doing this, but the savings outweigh the extra time spent.

I do get strange looks from prospective tenants. "Why isn't there any carpet?" or "Aren't you going to install carpet?" they ask.

I explain to them why I use tile and linoleum flooring, and they usually agree it's a good idea. For those who still like a little carpet, I suggest an area rug.

What Type of Heating/Cooling?

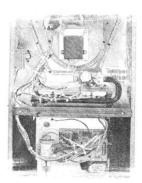

If heat is installed prior to your purchasing the rental property, the choice has been made for you. But if you want to make a change, here are a few things to keep in mind:

1. Are all the utilities (gas, electric, water, sewer) separated in this property?
2. Will the property require central air, or will windows or wall-mount air conditioning units work?
3. What was the last heat source? Gas furnace forced air, boiler, baseboard electric, baseboard hot water, fan forced electric?
4. Do you have access and funds to rewire some or all of the property?

You have to consider the necessary changes carefully. Any decision you make could require some sort of retrofitting.

Another question you need to ask is "Who pays the heating and cooling bills?"

If tenants are going to pay the utility bill you need to look for ease of conversion to a new heating/cooling system in addition to general cost-effectiveness.

If you, the landlord, are going to pay the bills, however, you need consider the cost-effectiveness of the system (installation and use) over the long-term, the next 20-years.

Garbage Disposal?

With all amenities, you need to consider the cost of upkeep and whether the tenant is likely to take care of it. In light of these two considerations, garbage disposals are often more of a headache than they are worth.

Do not assume tenants will place only proper items in the disposal. This is important: they won't. They will try to send everything possible down the disposal.

If you peel 20 potatoes for mashed potatoes at home, you'll put the peels in the trash. But in an apartment, you can be sure they'll be placed in the garbage disposal.

And, yes, they *will* plug it up.

Don't forget about spoons, forks, and knives, either. You can tell they're in the disposal by the awful racket they make. And no matter how long you run the disposal, no, they will *not* grind up.

But they will end up in the disposal anyway.

You also need to think of liability. When installed, the switch for the disposal needs to be far enough away so the person with his hand down the disposal can't turn it on.

(And now you're smiling because you know someone who would accidentally turn the disposal on while his hand was in it.)

The distance from switch to disposal should be at least seven feet. Not many people have a seven-foot wing span.

Ice Maker?

It might seem strange to ask whether you should get an ice maker when you purchase a refrigerator, but hear me out.

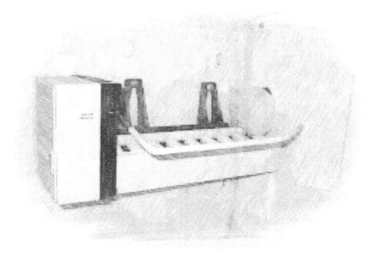

A refrigerator is pretty basic. There's the fridge and the freezer. There's a compressor, a fan, and a thermostat. There aren't many moving parts. I have had some refrigerators in apartments for 20 years. Once in awhile I need to replace the door shelves, but that's it.

A standard 18-19 cubic foot refrigerator, which is a great size for most units, costs about $400. For a house, I sometimes use a 23-cubic-foot model.

Now add an ice maker.

First, do you want to spend the money? It costs between $100 and $200 extra.

Second, do you have a water line to the location where the fridge will be? If not, purchase ice cube trays instead.

Third, do you want to spend $120 every three years to replace the ice cube maker? Without soft water, that's the life of an ice cube maker. With soft water, you can get another two years out of it.

Remember, if you have a water softener, but the tenant doesn't add salt on a regular schedule, you don't really have soft water.

I should add that if you don't know how to replace an ice cube maker, you can add another $125 for a service call.

See, the ice maker question *is* important.

Dish Washer?

A dish washer is another appliance with the potential to cause headaches.

I have 25 rental units and not one dishwasher among them. A few had dishwashers when I purchased them, but when the dishwashers failed, I replaced them with an additional 24" lower cabinet.

I don't like dishwashers because I've found tenants don't take care of them. They don't clean them. They don't pre-rinse dishes properly. They don't use proper detergent. And so on.

I've had too many dishwasher water issues in the past to ever consider installing one again.

And in the past 15 years, I have never had a prospective tenant ask if there was a dishwasher.

It's one of those appliances tenants don't seem to care about.

Storm Doors?

I'd like to have storm doors on every door of a rental unit. It allows the tenants to open the security door, get some fresh air in the unit, while providing a sense of security.

However, when a tenant moves in, he often removes the auto-closer and the chain at the top that keeps the door from over-extending when opening. That way it's easier to move furniture in. But most time I've found that they don't reinstall these two items. The storm doors now blow in the wind.

So the screens tear and the glass breaks.

When I first entered the rental business, I made sure every door had a storm door. After awhile, the storm doors became so damaged they were useless. I removed them and did not replace them.

It's just too expensive to replace storm doors every three to four years.

Conclusion

These are some of the choices I've made over the years. The goal is to provide a nice living space for your tenants without needing to repair and replace items unnecessarily. By considering these and other decisions like them, I've found more time to spend on the things that matter more than amenities no one misses.

25 - The Perfect Tenant

Back in May 2009, I met a potential tenant at a one-bedroom apartment I had for rent. He arrived alone, in a late model Bonneville, and he walked in with a cane. I introduced myself.

"Very nice to meet you." He spoke with a thick southern accent. "My name is Hassell P. Hall."

Little did I know this was the start of one of my most fulfilling relationships!

Hassell was retired and on Social Security. His wife was on disability due to a kidney issue and was on dialysis. Hassell treated her like a queen. He took great pleasure in providing for his wife through the good times and the bad.

When I showed him the apartment, he asked all the right questions before he filled out an application.

1. What type of heat is there?

2. Is the water heater gas or electric?

3. Is the stove gas or electric?

4. What utilities will I pay?

5. If maintenance needs done, who do I call?

6. Can we hang pictures?

7. Where is parking?

8. Do you require references?

9. Can I have guests stay here?

10. How are the neighbors?

After I answered these questions, he told me about his income and expenses, and I showed him all the features and amenities of the unit.

The unit did not have a washer/dryer hook-up. "Where's the closest laundry mat?" he asked.

"Only two blocks away."

"That's good."

This meant he did the laundry since his wife was not able to get out to do it.

Only after all this did he fill out the application. My standard checks were not going to bring up much.

1. Credit Check – This was not worth doing as his credit history was limited.

2. Background Check – This was not needed as both he and his wife were on Social Security.

3. Past Rental Experience – This was not available to me at the time.

So, based solely on my personal time with Hassell, I decided to rent to him.

He and his wife rented the apartment until April 2011, almost two full years. During the time he was there, he took care of his wife's every need. Twice a week, he took her to dialysis. He did the laundry, the cooking, and the cleaning.

Then, in March 2011, his wife passed away due to complications from her kidney treatments. He no longer felt right staying in the apartment.

So he moved out, not because of past due rent or unwanted guests or legal troubles, but because he loved his wife.

He decided to move in with a relative while he figured out what he wanted to do next. He left the apartment spotless. It was in as good condition as when he moved in. I returned his full deposit to him.

My wife and I attended the visitation. We were good acquaintances after two years and enjoyed Hassell and his wife.

A few months later, in August, Hassell called me.

"I am no longer comfortable living with my relative," he explained. "Would you have a place available that would fit my budget?"

"Actually, I think I do."

I had an efficiency apartment that would fit his needs perfectly. I met him at the apartment, showed it to him, and after he filled out an application, he became my tenant again in September 2012.

He remained in the unit until the end of his one-year lease. His daughter and son-in-law needed someone to watch their home because they were moving to Alabama, and he agreed to watch it while it was on the market.

I returned his full deposit once again. The apartment was in such good condition I could rent it out immediately.

His daughter's home sold quickly, and he decided to move to Alabama with them so he could spend more time with his grandkids.

Now, Hassell was a good ole Southern boy. It seems his daughter and son-in-law looked down on the people in Alabama, and this offended Hassel. Though he really enjoyed his time with his grandkids, after about eight months he decided to move back north.

I heard about his plan to return second-hand in February 2013 from Steve, a friend of his. "When Hassell's back in the area, have him call me," I told the friend. "I'll make sure I find something available in his price range."

When the call came, I had a nice one-bedroom apartment with full basement, washer/dryer hook-up, and carport. However, it was $375/month.

This was outside of Hassell's price range. He liked the apartment but just couldn't commit to the monthly rent.

"I'll tell you what," I told him. "If you keep an eye out on the neighboring apartments and watch the dumpster out back, I'll do $300 a month. I won't need a deposit, either. You've more than proven yourself to be an excellent tenant."

He agreed to the new price and signed the lease.

Hassell is a proud man. He's a veteran of the Korean War. He's experienced things in his lifetime I'll never truly understand and which has provided the opportunity for the life I have. Some tenants who are on Social Security get additional government assistance to help with bills. Hassell doesn't do that.

I once informed him about utility assistance from the county and about the local food pantry.

"There are others who need those things more than me," he said.

So, when he moved in, my wife and I decided to make sure he was stocked up on food and other items. Some friends of ours brought over furniture from their church. Cupboards stocked, rooms furnished, we had everything ready for him.

Below are some pictures from his move-in.

In November 2013, I invited Hassell to our family Thanksgiving celebration. He spent hours talking with my mother and my wife's parents and really enjoyed the evening.

We packed up some of the leftovers and sent it home with him. And, just as you would expect, he called a few days later. "I've cleaned the containers. You can pick them up at any time."

Thoughtful and courteous as always.

Hassell is still renting as of the time of this writing. When he moved in, he had no real possessions. Despite his meager means, Hassell has routinely gone out of his way to assist the other tenants in his building.

So whenever a tenant moved out and left items behind, I've asked Hassell if he would like any of them.

He has received silverware, dishes, furniture, a TV, and more pots and pans than one person could use. We're in the process of locating him a reliable vehicle and a washer and dryer.

In all my years of renting apartments, I have never met a man more true to his word or more filled with kindness.

Every once in a while I stop by his apartment just to visit. Many times while talking to him, he receives a phone call from his grandchildren. They call every day to ask Grandpa for advice, and he shares his wisdom and experiences, hoping to make them better people. He wants them to contribute to society rather than take from it.

I think everyone could learn something from Hassell. If everyone had his honesty, integrity, humility, heart, and sense of stewardship, the world would be a better place.

Appendices

Appendix 1 - 36 Things a Tenant Should Know

While this book deals primarily with landlord issues and experiences, it's important you know what areas tenants are being told to look into. If you don't have procedures for one of the following areas, you need to make one. Applicants and tenants have so much information available to them, you need to make sure you're properly informed and prepared.

If you want responsible, well-informed tenants, being a responsible, well-informed landlord is the first step.

SHOPPING AROUND

1. Check Out The Neighborhood

If you're moving to an area you already know or that's close to where you currently live, you have the luxury of visiting the area before you schedule an appointment to see the property. Check out the community and see if the amenities meet your expectations. If you enjoy eating out and nightlife, make sure you're not moving to a sleepy cul-de-sac far from the action. If you want a quiet neighborhood where your children can play, a house rental along a major road may be affordable and look good on paper, but isn't the best option.

Spend some time in the neighborhood. If it's a thriving community with shops and restaurants, stop in at a local cafe and chat up a friendly-looking employee. Let them know you're considering moving into the area and ask them what they think of the community. Sometimes, she may not live there herself, but in many cases you'll get someone who's willing to offer insight into what the neighborhood is really like.

If you can, stick around until after-hours or come back late in the evening and drive around. After the sun sets, you'll get a real feel for whether the neighborhood is safe at night, is as quiet (or as lively) as you hoped, or is somewhere you'd like to come home to after a long day of work.

2. Schedule a Visit With the Landlord

Depending on the rental market in your area, you may not have much time to waste when it comes to scheduling visits. When I gave up an apartment in the suburbs for a unit in the heart of the city, I quickly learned the rental market in my city's popular neighborhoods is brutal—apartments open and available on Monday could have a tenant moving in by Wednesday, and that's even if you scheduled a viewing on Tuesday. Don't waste time, but don't feel rushed either—new units come on the market regularly.

Call the landlord or property owner and ask them when he can meet with you, and if there are any regular tours scheduled or applications already in on the unit. This last bit is important— Don't waste your time visiting a unit where there's already an application unless you know you *have* to see it. Find out from the landlord how popular the property is and how likely it will be gone before you get there.

With Craigslist, a number of landlords prefer to do business over email or schedule group open houses. That's fine, but try to get them on the phone whenever possible. Speaking to someone gives you the opportunity to make your case and get immediate feedback, while email can get lost or be ignored for days on end.

3. Be Informed

Your first visit to an apartment may be your only visit before you submit an application, especially if the unit is in high demand. Don't waste the opportunity to ask your future landlord as many questions about the property as possible.

Ideally, you'll show up armed with the basics of the unit, which you can confirm with the property owner or landlord, if necessary. You'll already know how large the unit is, how much it costs, whether there's parking (assigned or not), and how close it is to your job, major roads, amenities, or mass transit. These are all things you can look up on the Internet before you go. Don't waste time during the visit on them.

4. Lease During the Slow-Season

Just like there's a purchase season for homes, there's a high- and low-season for renting. These seasons vary depending on location but typically follow demand.

For example, in northern states, high season is often in the summer or when college kids are scooping up apartments. Low season, on the other hand, ordinarily occurs during the winter.

With apartment leasing, as with most things, inventory dictates price, so your best bet is to lease your place during the low season. Not only will you have a greater variety of apartments available to choose from, but you'll be in a better position to negotiate price.

5. Take Notes

Don't rely on your memory. Take a lot of notes. If you are looking at multiple rental units, this will allow you to remember which landlord told you what.

What follows can guide you in asking more probing questions during your initial visit.

LEASE

6. Leases & Tenancies-At-Will

Your landlord may offer you a lease, which typically runs for one year, or a verbal or written tenancy-at-will agreement, which runs from month to month. A tenancy-at-will agreement gives you the opportunity to move out after giving the landlord a proper 30-day written notice, but it also allows the landlord to increase rent or to ask you to leave with a proper 30-day written notice. A lease offers you more security. Read the agreement completely before signing it. Keep a copy for your records.

7. Lease Length

Make sure you know the exact length of the lease--year, months, month-to-month, or other.

8. Conditions For Breaking Lease

As with any contract, there may be some reasons the landlord or property manager may let you out of a lease. Although these reasons are few and far between, make sure you know before you rent.

9. Roommates

If you have a lease, you will probably be responsible for paying the entire rent if a roommate moves out.

10. Evictions

If your landlord wants to evict you, he must terminate your tenancy with the proper written notice and then file a summary process action in court. Ultimately, only a judge can evict you. Make sure you respond to any court documents you receive. If you do not show up to defend yourself in court, you will lose by default.

RENT & OTHER FEES

11. Legal & Illegal Fees

When you move into an apartment, a landlord can charge you the first month's rent, your last month's rent, a security deposit, and a lock fee. A landlord may not charge you a broker's fee unless he is a licensed realtor.

12. Security Deposit & Last Month's Rent

Your landlord can legally require you to pay a security deposit and the last month's rent in amounts equivalent to one month's rent for each. If your landlord collects them, he must, among other things, give proper receipts.

13. Rent Payments

Make sure you know how much the rent is and when is it due, whether weekly, monthly, or quarterly.

14. Late Rent Fees and Returned Check Fees

Normally, rent is due on a specific day of the week or month. If rent is not delivered by that day, you will be subject to a late fee. There is usually no way around this. One thing you may not know is that if you send in a check and the check gets denied by your bank, then you will have to pay a "Returned Check Fee" to the landlord. You will now owe the late rent fee *and* the returned check fee.

15. Other up-front costs.

Are there any additional up-front cost other than the security deposit and the first and/or last month's rent? If there are, make sure they are itemize and that you receive an explanation of what those fees will be used for. Also, make sure your receipt reflects those additional fees.

16. Utilities

Determine which utilities you are responsible for. This is important because sometimes the utilities can cost as much as the rent. The landlord may be discounting the monthly rent due to extremely high utility costs.

Ask the landlord what the typical or average costs are for each utility you will be responsible for. If the landlord does not know, ask who the utility providers are and call those providers. Let them know you are interested in renting the unit and would like to know what the average utility costs were for the past 12 months. Most utility providers will give you this information.

17. Rent Increases

Ask the property manager or landlord what the typical rent increases have been over the past two to three years. If you are planning to stay a while, you will want to know if rent increases are automatic every time you sign a new lease, and the approximate increase you might expect.

18. When Money is Scarce, Talk to Your Landlord.

This tactic doesn't work if you spent your rent money at the mall, bar, or casino. But if you're truly strapped for cash, talk to your landlord. There's no guarantee a landlord can or will help, but if you don't ask, you never give him the opportunity to help. If you've experienced a hardship, your landlord may be willing to work out a payment plan, cut you some slack on your rent payment due date, or help you get into an apartment that's better suited for your situation.

THE APARTMENT

19. Condition of Apartment

Before entering a rental agreement, check out the condition of the apartment. If you can't, have a friend do it for you. You do not want to be charged for damages that existed when you moved in!

20. Code Violations

You are entitled to an apartment that is in compliance with local and state sanitary and building codes. Violations should be reported to your landlord in writing.

21. Turnover Rate

Does the building you are going to rent have a higher than usual turnover rate? Typically, tenants stay in an apartment two to three years if the service is acceptable. If the turnover rate is yearly, there may be an issue with either the landlord's service, or the rent increases being too high.

22. Painted and Cleaned

Sometimes landlords will forego cleaning an apartment and consider a lower security deposit. If this is the case, stay away from the rental unit. All landlords know having an apartment cleaned when someone moves out is part of the landlord's responsibilities.

As far as painting goes, sometimes the walls just need a good wipe down; other times, they will need repainted. Ask what was done prior to moving in.

23. Included Appliances

If appliances are included in the lease, then maintenance on those appliances should also be included. Consider the following when signing a lease:

- Refrigerator
- Oven/Stove
- Microwave
- Dishwasher
- Garbage Disposal
- In-Unit Washer and Dryer
- Laundry Facility on the property

24. Internet Service Providers

Ask you landlord who the Internet service providers are in the area.

25. Renter's Insurance

You have probably invested more in personal property than you realize. Computers, iPods, TVs, clothing, jewelry, cell phones, and furniture are expensive to replace in case of fire or theft. Renter's insurance is a good idea and can be surprisingly affordable.

26. Quiet Hours

If there are set times designated as "Quiet Hours," you will want to know these prior to moving in.

27. Noise

Be considerate of your neighbors. Having loud parties at night or cranking up the music may lead to complaints and, eventually, to eviction.

28. Complaints and Maintenance

You need to know the procedure for complaints and maintenance issues. It is preferable when the maintenance staff lives on the premises.

29. Responsibility for Basic Upkeep

You need to know who is responsible for replacing the following:

- Furnace Filters
- Light Bulbs
- Smoke Detection Batteries
- Carbon Monoxide Detector Batteries

A landlord or property manager may tell you that it is your responsibility, but that you can call them to change them for a fee. This fee usually covers the cost of material plus labor.

30. Responsibility for Pest Control

Often, large communities and condominiums have a contract with a pest control firm that works with their residents. The property manager may send them out to you when you request their help, or you may simply be required to use their services instead of another company's.

Other times, though, landlords leave the responsibility for pest control to the tenant, unless there's some kind of pre-existing condition when they move into the unit. I've seen leases that say after the first 30 days, a tenant is on his own when it comes to pest control. Ask the landlord on your first viewing if there have been pest problems, and if so, who they use for pest control.

TENANT'S RIGHTS

31. Right of Privacy

While you may just be renting or leasing the property, you still have a right to privacy. This means your landlord cannot enter the premises whenever s/he pleases.

32. Landlord Notice

Landlords can enter rented premises only in the following circumstances:

- to show the property to prospective new tenants or purchasers

- to make needed repairs or (in some states) to determine

whether repairs are necessary

- in cases of emergency

Normally, a landlord will not enter a rental unit without the prior consent of a tenant. You can always ask existing tenants if they have ever found this not to be the case.

There are exceptions to this basic rule.

For instance, if you are renting the upstairs apartment of a duplex, and the downstairs tenant calls the landlord because their "roof" is leaking, that's actually your floor. The landlord may try to contact you, and if he cannot reach you, he may enter the apartment to determine what is leaking. If it is an easy fix, great. If this is a more complicated fix, he should contact you to make arrangements for repairs.

If a landlord or maintenance person enters your rental unit while you are absent, he should leave a copy of the work order so you know someone was in your rental unit.

Several states also allow landlords or property managers the right of entry during a tenant's extended absence, often defined as seven days or more, to maintain the property as necessary and to inspect for damage and needed repairs. In most cases, a landlord _may not_ enter just to check up on the tenant and the rental property.

States that regulate landlords' access require landlords to provide advance notice (usually 24 hours) before entering a rental unit. In most states, if a landlord does not give advance notice, he may enter rented premises while a tenant is living there only in an emergency—such as a fire or serious water leak—or when the tenant gives permission.

Be sure to know your state's specific rules.

33. Evictions - Types

An eviction is a legal process to remove someone from a residential or commercial property. In most situations, an eviction requires the involvement of the courts. If a landlord wishes to evict a tenant, he must follow the strict procedural rules of the state and, if in a rent-controlled market, the rules of the city. Some common types of eviction notices are:

- *Pay or Quit:* A pay or quit notice is used when the tenant has not paid rent. The landlord then warns the tenant that if he does not pay, he will be required to leave.

- *Cure or Quit:* A cure or quit notice is used when the tenant has violated another term of the lease. The landlord warns the tenant that if he does not fix the violation, he will be required to leave.

- *Unconditional Quit:* A tenant is ordered to move out within a certain period of time under the unconditional quit notice. The tenant is not offered the opportunity to fix any problems.

34. Fair Housing Laws

In addition to knowing about the eviction process, tenants should also know their rights with regards to Equal Housing Opportunities.

Equal Housing Opportunity

Property owners and managers are subject to the federal Fair Housing Act, which prohibits "any preference, limitation, or discrimination because of race, color, religion, sex, handicap, familial status, or national origin, or intention to make such preference, limitation or discrimination."

All landlords and property managers should support Equal Housing Opportunity and encourage everyone to follow appropriate guidelines to comply with both the Federal Housing Act, as well as any applicable state and local regulations. All property rental offers are available on an equal opportunity basis

Moreover, a property owner or manager cannot establish discriminatory terms or conditions in the purchase or rental, deny that housing is available, or advertise that the property is available only to persons of a certain race, color, religion, sex, handicap, familial status, or national original.

Renter's Rights

As someone seeking to rent an apartment, home or condo, you have the right to expect that housing will be available to you without discrimination or other limitations based on race, color, religion, sex, handicap, familial status, or national origin. This includes the right to expect equal professional service, the opportunity to consider a broad range of housing choices, no discriminatory limitations on communities or locations of housing, no discrimination in the pricing or financing of housing, reasonable accommodations in rules, practices and procedures for persons with disabilities, and to be free from harassment or intimidation for exercising your fair housing rights.

<u>The Law</u>

Civil Rights Act of 1866

The Civil Rights Act of 1866 prohibits all racial discrimination in the sale or rental of property.

The Fair Housing Act

The Fair Housing Act declares a national policy of fair housing throughout the United States, making illegal any discrimination in the sale, lease or rental of housing, or making housing otherwise unavailable, because of race, color, religion, sex, handicap, familial status, or national origin.

Americans with Disabilities Act

Title III of the Americans with Disabilities Act prohibits discrimination against persons with disabilities in places of public accommodations and commercial facilities.

The Equal Credit Opportunity Act

The Equal Credit Opportunity Act makes discrimination unlawful with respect to any aspect of a credit application on the basis of race, color, religion, national origin, sex, marital status, age or because all or part of the applicant's income derives from any public assistance program.

State and Local Laws

State and local laws often provide broader coverage and prohibit discrimination based on additional classes not covered by federal law.

35. Tax Benefits.

Many states offer a "Renter's Credit" or "Homestead Property Tax Credit" when you do your income taxes. The credit is typically based on the difference between your household income and property taxes. As a renter, you may not directly pay property taxes, but your landlord does, and those taxes are figured into your monthly rent payment. Make sure you hang onto any receipts showing paid rent so you can provide the IRS with documentation should they request it.

36. Be a Defensive Renter

A defensive renter is someone who acts as though there might be problems down the road -- and prepares for those problems. Here are some tips:

- Keep records of what happens between you and your landlord.

- Keep all letters, your lease, and rental receipts.

- Always pay by check or money order.

- Only pay in cash if you absolutely have to. If you pay in cash, insist on getting a signed receipt. If the receipt doesn't say exactly what you are paying for and how much, don't give up the cash.

- Never give the landlord title to your car and never sign over any check to a landlord. Pay him separately

- Report all problems immediately, in writing, to your landlord. If the problems continue and are serious, call the building inspector or health department.

- If you and your landlord decide to change anything about when you pay or how much, make sure that the agreement is in writing.

This is a general overview designed to avoid later problems. You should never hesitate to question your landlord. If you are still unsure about something, contact a lawyer or other qualified person. Because some landlords want to make as much money as possible from you without maintaining the property, you must be careful. Be a defensive renter.

~~~

These are the typical things tenants are being asked to be aware of. As landlords and property managers, we need to know the things a tenant might ask or expect and have answers ready.

If you are not sure how to answer these questions, you can always contact Real Tenant History and consult with one of our

Customer Service Representatives. In the event they are not able to help, they will point you in the right direction.

Appendix 2 – Small Claims Process (Indiana)

Rule 1. Scope; citation

(A)   Scope. These rules shall apply to all small claims proceedings in all courts of the State of Indiana, including {County} County Small Claims Courts, having jurisdiction over small claims as defined by relevant Indiana statutes.

(B) Citation. These rules may be cited as S.C. _____.

Rule 2. Commencement of Action

(A)   In General. An action under these rules shall be commenced by the filing of an unverified notice of claim in a court of competent jurisdiction and by payment of the prescribed filing fee or filing an order waiving the filing fee.

(B) Form of Notice of Claim. The notice of claim shall contain:

> (1)   The name, street address, and telephone number of the court;

> (2)   The name, address, and telephone number of the claimant and defendant(s);

> (3)   The place, date, and time when the parties are to appear on the claim, which date shall be set by the court with the objective of dispensing speedy justice between the parties according to the rules of substantive law;

> (4)   A brief statement of the nature and amount of the claim; and

>> (a)   If the claim arises out of written contract, a copy shall be attached; however, the fact that a copy of such contract is not in the custody of

the plaintiff shall not bar the filing of the claim; and

(b) If the claim is on an account, an Affidavit of Debt, in a form substantially similar to Small Claims Appendix A shall be attached;

(5) A statement that the parties may appear either in person or by an attorney;

(6) An instruction to the defendant that the defendant should bring to the trial all documents in the possession of or under the control of the defendant concerning the claim;

(7) A statement that if the defendant does not wish to dispute the claim he may nonetheless appear for the purpose of allowing the court to establish the method by which the judgment shall be paid;

(8) The name, street address and telephone number of the person designated by the court with whom the defendant may communicate if defendant is unable to appear at the time or place designated in the notice;

(9) A statement that a default judgment may be entered against the defendant if he fails to appear on the date specified in the notice of the claim;

(10) Notice of the defendant's right to a jury trial and that such right is waived unless a jury trial is requested within ten (10) days after receipt of the notice of claim; that once a jury trial request has been granted, it may not be withdrawn without the consent of the other party or parties; and within ten (10) days after the jury trial request has been granted, the party requesting a

jury trial shall pay the clerk the additional amount required by statute to transfer the claim to the plenary docket or, in the {County} Small Claims Court, the filing fee necessary to file a case in the appropriate court of the county; otherwise, the party requesting a jury trial shall be deemed to have waived the request; and

(11) Any additional information which may facilitate proper service.

(C) Assistance by Clerk. The clerk of the court shall prepare and furnish blank notice of claim forms and the clerk of the court, or other employee of the court as the judge may designate, shall, upon request, assist individual claimants in the preparation thereof, but all attachments to the notice of claim shall be furnished by the claimant.

(D) Number of Claims and Attachments. All claims and attachments thereto shall be filed in such quantity that one copy may remain on file with the clerk, one copy may be delivered to the claimant, and one copy may be served on each defendant.

(E) Documents and Information Excluded from Public Access and Confidential Pursuant to Administrative Rule 9(G)(1). Documents and information excluded from public access pursuant to Administrative Rule 9(G)(1) shall be filed in accordance with Trial Rule 5(G).

Rule 3. Manner of service

(A) General Provision. For the purpose of service the notice of claim shall also be considered to be the summons. A copy of the notice of claim shall be served upon each defendant. Service may be made by sending a copy by certified mail with return receipt requested, or by delivering a copy to the defendant personally, or by leaving a copy at the defendant's dwelling house or usual place of abode, or in any other manner provided in Trial Rules 4.1 through 4.16. Whenever service is made by leaving a copy at defendant's dwelling house or usual place of abode, the person making the service also shall send by first class mail a copy of the notice of claim to the last known address of the person being served.

(B) Designation of Constable in the {County} County Small Claims Court. Pursuant to Trial Rule 4.12, the {County} County Small Claims Court judge may appoint the elected township constable and deputies as the persons specifically designated by the court to effect service in person. An order with the names of the respective constable and deputies shall be entered in the Record of Judgments and Orders of the particular division of the Small Claims Court.

(C) Designation of Manner of Service in the {County} County Small Claims Court. A person seeking service of a notice of claim filed in the {County} County Small Claims Court, or his or her attorney, may designate upon the notice of claim the manner of service as either in person by the constable or by certified mail or other public means by which a written acknowledgment of receipt may be requested and obtained, as provided in Trial Rule 4.1. The judge of a {County} County Small Claims Court may designate by order an employee as bailiff for the purpose of effecting service of process by certified mail and collecting appropriate fees. If the manner of service is not designated by the person seeking service, the clerk of the court shall note such absence on the notice of claim and shall promptly deliver the notice of claim to the employee appointed by the court as bailiff or to the constable for service by certified mail. The cost for service is set by legislation, and there shall be no additional charge for first class mail delivery required pursuant to T.R. 4.1(B).

(D) Return of Service. The person making service shall comply promptly with the provisions of Trial Rule 4.15. In addition, he or she shall state on the return of service if service was made by delivering a copy to a person, naming such person, or by leaving a copy at the defendant's dwelling or abode, describing the dwelling or abode and noting any unique features, and shall verify that a copy of the notice of claim was sent by first class mail and indicate the address to which the notice was sent. The clerk of court shall note the return of service on the Chronological Case Summary applicable to the case.

Rule 4. Responsive pleadings

(A)   Preservation of Defenses. All defenses shall be deemed at issue without responsive pleadings, but this provision shall not alter the burden of proof.

(B)   Entry of Appearance. For the purpose of administrative convenience the court may request that the defendant enter an appearance prior to trial. Such appearance may be made in person, by telephone or by mail but the fact that no appearance is entered by the defendant shall not be grounds for default judgment.

Rule 5. Counterclaims

(A)   Time and Manner of Filing. If the defendant has any claim against the plaintiff, the defendant may bring or mail a statement of such claim to the small claims court within such time as will allow the court to mail a copy to the plaintiff and be received by the plaintiff at least seven (7) calendar days prior to the trial. If such counterclaim is not received within this time the plaintiff may request a continuance pursuant to S.C. 9. The counterclaim must conform with the requirements of S.C. 2(B)(4).

(B) Counterclaim in Excess of Jurisdiction. Any defendant pursuing a counterclaim to decision waives the excess of the defendant's claim over the jurisdictional maximum of the small claims docket and may not later bring a separate action for the remainder of such claim.

Rule 6. Discovery

Discovery may be had in a manner generally pursuant to the rules governing any other civil action, but only upon the approval of the court and under such limitations as may be specified. The court should grant discovery only upon notice and good cause shown and should limit such action to the necessities of the case.

Rule 7. Pretrial settlement

All settlements shall be in writing and signed by the plaintiff and defendant. The settlement shall be filed with the clerk and upon approval of the court it shall be entered in the small claims judgment docket and shall have the same effect as a judgment of the court.

Rule 8. Informality of Hearing

(A) Procedure. The trial shall be informal, with the sole objective of dispensing speedy justice between the parties according to the rules of substantive law, and shall not be bound by the statutory provisions or rules of practice, procedure, pleadings or evidence except provisions relating to privileged communications and offers of compromise.

(B) Witnesses. All testimony shall be given under oath or affirmation. Witnesses may be called and the court shall have the power to issue subpoenas to compel their attendance. There shall be no additional fee charged for the issuance of subpoenas.

(C)   Appearance. Any assigned or purchased claim, or any debt acquired from the real party in interest by a third party cannot be presented or defended by said third party unless this third party is represented by counsel. In all other cases, the following rules shall apply:

>   (1)   Natural Persons. A natural person may appear pro se or by counsel in any small claims proceeding.

>   (2)   Sole Proprietorship and Partnerships. A sole proprietor or partnership may appear by a designated full-time employee of the business in the presentation or defense of claims arising out of the business, if the claim does not exceed one thousand five hundred dollars ($1,500.00). However, claims exceeding one thousand five hundred dollars ($1,500.00) must either be defended or presented by counsel or pro se by the sole proprietor or a partner.

>   (3)   Corporate Entities, Limited Liability Companies (LLC's), Limited Liability Partnerships (LLP's). All corporate entities, Limited Liability Companies (LLC's), and Limited Liability Partnerships (LLP's) may appear by a designated full-time employee of the corporate entity in the presentation or defense of claims arising out of the business if the claim does not exceed one thousand five hundred dollars ($1,500.00). However, claims exceeding one thousand five hundred dollars ($1,500.00) must be defended or presented by counsel.

>   (4)   Full-Time Employee Designations--Binding Effect of esignations and Requirements.

>>   (a)   In the event a corporate entity, sole proprietorship, partnership, LLC or LLP

designates a full-time employee to appear in its stead, the corporate entity, sole proprietor, partnership, LLC or LLP will be bound by any and all agreements relating to the small claims proceedings entered into by the designated employee and will be liable for any and all costs, including those assessed by reason of contempt, levied by a court against the designated employee.

(b)   By authorizing a designated full-time employee to appear under this Rule, the corporate entity, sole proprietorship, partnership, LLC or LLP waives any present or future claim in this or any other forum in excess of one thousand five hundred dollars ($1,500.00.

(c)   No person who is disbarred or suspended from the practice of law in Indiana or any other jurisdiction may appear for a corporate entity or on behalf of a sole proprietor, partnership, LLC or LLP under this rule.

(5)   Full-Time Employee Designations--Contents. Before a designated employee is allowed to appear in a small claims proceeding, the corporate entity, sole proprietorship, partnership, LLC or LLP must have on file with the court exercising jurisdiction of the proceedings, a certificate of compliance with the provisions of this rule, wherein the corporate entity, sole proprietorship, partnership, LLC or LLP must expressly accept, by a duly adopted resolution in the case of a corporate entity, LLC or LLP; or a document signed under oath by the sole proprietor or managing partner of a partnership, the binding character of the designated employee's acts,

the liability of the corporate entity, sole proprietorship, partnership, LLC or LLP for assessments and costs levied by a court, and that the corporate entity, sole proprietorship, partnership, LLC or LLP waives any claim for damages in excess of one thousand five hundred dollars ($1,500.00) associated with the facts and circumstances alleged in the notice of claim. Additionally, the designated employee must have on file with the court exercising jurisdiction of the proceedings an affidavit stating that he/she is not disbarred or suspended from the practice of law in Indiana or any other jurisdiction.

Rule 9. Continuances

(A)   Either party may be granted a continuance for good cause shown. Except in unusual circumstances no party shall be allowed more than one (1) continuance in any case, and all continuances must have the specific approval of the court. Continuances shall be for as short a period as possible, and where feasible the party not requesting the continuance shall be considered in scheduling a new hearing date. The court shall give notice of the continuance and the new date and time of trial to all parties.

(B)   Designating Employee. The court may, by a duly executed order recorded in the Record of Judgments and Orders, designate a specifically named employee to be responsible for scheduling hearings under specific directions spelled out by the court in said order.

Rule 10. Dismissal and default

(A)   Dismissal. If the plaintiff fails to appear at the time and place specified in the notice of claim, or for any continuance thereof, the court may dismiss the action without prejudice. If a counterclaim has been filed the court may grant judgment for the defendant after first making an inquiry similar to that required by S.C. 10(B) in the case of default judgments. If the claim is refiled and the plaintiff again fails to appear such claim may be dismissed with prejudice.

(B)   Default. If the defendant fails to appear at the time and place specified in the notice of claim, or for any continuance thereof, the court may enter a default judgment against him. Before default judgment is entered, the court shall examine the notice of claim and return thereof and make inquiry, under oath, of those present so as to assure the court that:

> (1)   Service of notice of claim was had under such circumstances as to establish a reasonable probability that the defendant received such notice;

> (2)   Within the knowledge of those present, the defendant is not under legal disability and has sufficient understanding to realize the nature and effect of the notice of claim;

> (3)   Either (a) the defendant is not entitled to the protections against default judgments provided by the Service members Civil Relief Act, as amended (the "Act"), 50 U.S.C. appx. § 521, or (b) the plaintiff has filed with the court, subscribed and certified or declared to be true under penalty of perjury, the affidavit required by the Act (i) stating whether or not the defendant is in military service and showing necessary facts to support the affidavit; or (ii) if the plaintiff is unable to determine whether or not the defendant is in military service, stating that the plaintiff is unable to determine whether or not the defendant is in military service; and

> (4)   The plaintiff has a prima facie case.

After such assurance, the court may render default judgment and, upon entering such judgment, shall assess court costs against the defendant.

(C) Setting Aside Default. Upon good cause shown the court may, within one year after entering a default judgment, vacate such judgment and reschedule the hearing of the original claim. Following the expiration of one year, the judgment debtor may seek a reversal of the original judgment only upon the filing of an independent action, as provided in Ind.R.Tr.P. 60(B).

Rule 11. Judgment

(A) Entry and Notice of Judgment. All judgments shall be reduced to writing signed by the court, dated, entered in the Record of Judgments and Orders, and noted in the small claims judgment docket and the Chronological Case Summary. The {County} County Small Claims Court shall forward its judgments to the Clerk of the Circuit Court of {County} County for entry on the {County} County judgment docket. Judgment shall be subject to review as prescribed by relevant Indiana rules and statutes. Notwithstanding the provisions of T.R. 5(A), the court shall send notice of all small claims judgments and all judgments of the {County} County Small Claims Court, whether by default or not, to the attorneys of record, or if a party is appearing pro se, to the party of record.

(B) Costs. The party recovering judgment shall also recover costs regardless of the amount.

(C) Method of Payment. Modification. The court may order a judgment paid the prevailing party in any specified manner. If the judgment is not paid as ordered the court may modify its payment order as it deems necessary.

The judgment creditor may seek enforcement of his judgment by any other method provided by law.

(D) Release of Judgment. Upon payment in full, including accrued interest, the clerk shall notify the judgment creditor and shall require him or her to file a release of judgment. If the judgment creditor fails to file a release of judgment within thirty (30) days of the issuance of the notice, the clerk shall note in the Chronological Case Summary that the judgment has been satisfied and that the plaintiff has failed to release judgment pursuant to court directive, and the clerk shall note a release of judgment in the judgment docket.

(E) Deleted, eff. Jan. 1, 1990.

(F) Effect of Judgment. A judgment shall be res judicata only as to the amount involved in the particular action and shall not be considered an adjudication of any fact at issue in any other action or court.

Rule 12. Venue

(A) Proper Venue.

> (1) Proper venue for a case filed in the small claims docket of a Circuit or Superior Court shall be in the county where the transaction or occurrence took place, where the obligation was incurred or is to be performed, or where a defendant resides or is employed at the time the complaint is filed.

> (2) Except as provided in (3) below, proper venue for a case filed in a small claims court created pursuant to IC 33-34-1-2 shall be in the township where the transaction or occurrence took place, where the obligation was incurred or is to be performed, or where

a defendant resides or is employed at the time the complaint is filed.

(3)   Proper venue of any claim between landlord and tenant, including but not limited to a claim for rent, possession of real estate, return of property, return of security deposit or for damages, filed in a small claims court created pursuant to IC 33-34-1-2 shall be in the township where the real estate is located, unless there is no small claims court in that township.

(B) Motion to Correct Venue. When it appears that the county or township, in the case of small claims courts created pursuant to IC 33-34-1-2 in which the action is pending is not the proper place for the hearing of such action, the court shall, on the motion of a party or upon its own motion, determine the correctness of the venue. If the venue is incorrect the judge shall, at the option of the plaintiff, order the action to be transferred or dismissed without prejudice unless the defendant appears and waives the venue requirement.

(C)   No Waiver of Venue. No contract or agreement shall operate as a waiver of the provisions of this rule and the court shall treat any such attempt as being void.

Rule 13. Small claims litigant's manual

An informative small claims manual shall be formulated by the Judicial Conference of Indiana for distribution to the small claims courts. Each county shall reproduce such manual and shall make it available to every litigant and to such other persons or organizations as the court may deem appropriate.

Rule 14. Appointment of referee by circuit judge; compensation

In any circuit court exercising small claims jurisdiction, the circuit judge may appoint a referee to assist the court in performing the "county court functions." Such referee shall be an attorney admitted to practice in Indiana and shall serve at the pleasure of the circuit judge. The referee shall have such authority as the circuit judge shall assign by order. The referee shall be a finder of fact--the decision rendered will be that of the circuit judge.

Such referee shall be paid reasonable compensation, including a mileage allowance to be determined by the appointing circuit court judge. In recommending to the Supreme Court of Indiana appropriate compensation, the appointing circuit court judge shall consider the estimated caseload, the amount of work time needed to fulfill the assigned duties, and any other relevant factors relating to the referee's duties. Compensation shall be reasonably commensurate with the workload assigned. The amount authorized by the Supreme Court to be paid shall be paid by the state.

Rule 15. Method of Keeping Records

Under the direction of the Supreme Court of Indiana, the Clerk of the Circuit Court may, notwithstanding the recordkeeping practices set forth for small claims proceedings, keep records in any suitable media. The recordkeeping formats and systems and the quality and permanency requirements employed for the Chronological Case Summary, the Case File, and the Record of Judgments and Orders (Order Book) shall be approved by the Division of State Court Administration for compliance with applicable requirements.

Rule 16. Order of Possession of Real Estate

(A)   Time for Requesting. An order of possession of real estate shall not be issued if more than thirty (30) days have passed since the judgment was issued. Thereafter, a plaintiff seeking possession may do so by filing a new case.

(B)   Duration. An order of possession of real estate shall be effective for no more than thirty (30) consecutive days after its date of issue. The court shall indicate the specific date of expiration on the face of each order of possession.

Source: (http://www.in.gov)

{County} = County Name

~~~

If you would like to review the small claims process for other states, please visit the "Resources" section at Real Tenant History (www.realtenanthistory.com).

Appendix 3 – Lease Addendums

Over the past few years, it has become common to add a lease addendum to the regular lease.

A standard lease covers the most important aspects of renting an apartment or house, so instead of modifying the standard lease for special cases, many landlords will add an addendum as a separate document to sign.

While this addendum is part of the lease, it is sometimes viewed as a separate contract.

Over the past few years, we have seen addendums for the following areas become popular.

- **Crime Free Lease Addendum (Indiana)**

- **Bed Bug Lease Addendum (Indiana)**

Crime Free lease Addendum (Sample Indiana)

In consideration of the execution or renewal of a lease of the dwelling unit identified in the lease, Lessor and Lessee agree that the Lessee, and any member of the Lessee's household or a guest or other person under the Lessee's control, shall not engage in criminal activity including the following:

1. DRUG-RELATED CRIMINAL ACTIVITY, ON OR NEAR THE SAID PREMISES. Drug-related criminal activity means the illegal manufacture, sale, distribution, use or possession with intent to manufacture, sell, distribute, or use a controlled substance (as defined in Section 102 of the controlled Substance Act 21 U.S.C. 802)

2. ENGAGE IN ANY ACT INTENDED TO FACILITATE CRIMINAL ACTIVITY, including drug-related criminal activity, on or near said premises.

3. PERMITTING THE DWELLING UNIT TO BE USED FOR, OR TO FACILITATE CRIMINAL ACTIVITY, including drug-related criminal activity, regardless of whether the individual engaging in such activity is a member of the household or a guest.

4. UNLAWFUL MANUFACTURING, SELLING, USING, STORING, OR KEEPING OR GIVING OF A CONTROLLED SUBSTANCE as defined in I.C. 35-489, at any location, whether on or near the dwelling unit or otherwise.

5. PROSTITUTION, as defined in IC 35-45-4-2, CRIMINAL STREET GANG ACTIVITY as defined in IC 35-45-9-1, THREATENING OR INTIMIDATING as prohibited by IC 34-45-2-1. BATTERY as prohibited in IC 35-45-2-1, including but not limited to the UNLAWFUL DISCHARGE OF FIREARMS, on or near the dwelling unit premises, or breach of the lease agreement that otherwise jeopardizes the health, safety, and welfare of the landlord, his agent of their tenants or involving imminent or actual serious property damage.

Violation of the above provisions shall be a material and irreparable violation of the lease and good cause for termination of tenancy. A single violation of any provision of this added addendum shall be deemed a serious violation and a material and irreparable noncompliance.

It is understood that a SINGLE VIOLATION shall be good cause for immediate termination of the lease unless otherwise provided by law, proof of violation shall not require criminal conviction, but shall be a preponderance of the evidence.

In case of conflict between provisions of this addendum and any other provisions of the lease, the provisions of the addendum shall govern.

This lease addendum is incorporated into the lease executed or renewed this date between Lessor and Lessee herein referenced by Lessor (As Owner) and Lessee.

Signature: _____ Date: _____

Signature: _____ Date: _____

Bed Bug Lease Addendum - Background

So What is a Bed Bud?

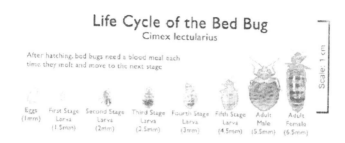

Life Cycle of the Bed Bug
Cimex lectularius

After hatching, bed bugs need a blood meal each
time they molt and move to the next stage

| Eggs (1mm) | First Stage Larva (1.5mm) | Second Stage Larva (2mm) | Third Stage Larva (2.5mm) | Fourth Stage Larva (3mm) | Fifth Stage Larva (4.5mm) | Adult Male (5.5mm) | Adult Female (6.5mm) |

Scale: 1 cm

Bed bugs, or cimex lectularius, have existed since humans lived in caves. These small wingless insects feed on human blood and typically bite during the night. Fully grown adult bed bugs are about the size of apple seeds. Eggs and newborns are very small and usually whitish in color. The color, and to a degree, shape, of older bed bugs can vary depending how long it's been since their last meal. Females usually have rounder back ends, while males have a somewhat pointier back ends.

Although they're called bed bugs, the name is a misleading since they can be found in couches, chairs, clock radios, or anywhere you can find their food source: people. They are literally "out for blood" and will go wherever people go. Since bed bugs don't fly, they spread by hitch-hiking on people or their belongings, like luggage, clothing, and purses.

Bed Bug Lease Addendum – Reasons

The Bed Bug Addendum is relatively new for the rental business. This is because people in general are more mobile and may spend the night elsewhere more often than in the past, as well as spending more time in hotels for business. This has increased the incidence of bed bugs in rental units.

Bed Bug Lease Addendum - Sample – Indiana

Bed Bugs have become common throughout the United States. They are a growing problem and are present in Indiana. They can invade your residence from many different sources. We need your help to prevent them and, if an infestation occurs, we need you to notify us immediately. Do not attempt to treat them yourself. It requires a professional and immediate action is extremely important to control an infestation. Any delay will make the problem much worse. Lack of cooperation and immediate reporting of bed bugs will result in the immediate termination of tenancy.

This Bed Bug Addendum ("Addendum") is entered into this _____ day of _____, 20__,

between _____ ("Lessor")

and _____ ("Lesser").

This is related to the lease of the following premises: _____ (The "Unit").

1. Resident agrees that they are aware of the negative impact bed bug infestations can have on the personal enjoyment of all residents in the community or rental property and will cooperate with "Lessor" to carry out the terms of this addendum. Lack of cooperation will result in the immediate termination of tenancy.

2. The Lessor:

   2.a. ____ has not inspected the unit specifically for bed bugs, but is unaware of any infestation.

   2.b. ____ is not aware of any infestation as of the date the unit was last inspected on ___/___/___.

3. Resident states that Resident will personally inspect the unit before or immediately after move-in and will immediately report any signs of bed bugs.

4. Resident states that all furniture and personal belongings to be moved into the unit are free of bed bugs.

5. Resident agrees to prevent possible infestation by following the list of responsibilities for the duration of tenancy:

   5.a. Resident will check for bed bug infestation by inspecting the unit after guest visits;

   5.b. Resident shall check clothing, luggage, backpacks, shoes and other personal belonging for signs of bed bugs before re-entering the unit after staying in a hotel or other home, visiting a theater, using public transportation, or any other place that may have bed bugs.

   5.c. Resident shall inspect all used furniture items and rental furniture items for infestation before moving them into the unit, and shall not move items into the unit if any bed bugs or signs of bed bugs are found.

6. Resident agrees to take the following steps once an infestation is suspected or discovered in Resident's unit or any adjoining unit:

> 6.a. Resident shall report any suspected infestation immediately to Lessor;
>
> 6.b. Resident shall grant "Lessor" or his agent access to the unit for inspection within 24 hours of making the report;
>
> 6.c. Resident shall cooperate with all pest control efforts and instructions from the lessor's pest control professional;
>
> 6.d. Resident shall not try to resolve the problem by treating the infestation with products available at stores;
>
> 6.e. Resident shall allow Lessor's licensed pest control professional to inspect the unit and treat the unit using their recommended protocols;
>
> 6.f. Resident shall accept Lessor's licensed pest control professional's recommendations and dispose of any furnishings or personal items that are not salvageable by sealing them in plastic and removing then from the unit as instructed by the professional;
>
> 6.g. Resident shall place all beddings, drapes, curtains and small rugs in plastics bags for transport to laundry or dry cleaners;
>
> 6.h. Resident shall empty all dressers, night stands and closets;

6.i. Resident shall remove all items from floors;

6.j. Resident shall bag all clothing, shoes, boxes, toys, etc, separating washable from non-washable items;

6.k. Resident shall wash all machine washable bedding, drapes, clothing, etc, on the hottest water temperature and dry on the hottest heat setting;

6.l. Resident shall take all non-washable items to a dry cleaner and shall inform the dry cleaner of the issue for proper cleaning and Resident's expense;

6.m. Resident shall safely dispose of all items that cannot be decontaminated;

6.n. Resident shall vacuum all floors including the inside of closets, all furniture including the inside of drawers and nightstands, mattresses and box springs;

6.o. Resident shall dispose of all plastics bags used for transporting items for cleaning;

6.p. Resident shall dislodge bed bug eggs by using a brush attachment;

6.q. Resident shall remove all vacuum bags and seal them tightly in plastic and discard them properly;

6.r. Resident shall move furniture toward the center of the room so licensed pest control professional can easily treat carpet edges, walls, and furniture surfaces;

6.s. Resident understand that they licensed pest control professional may recommend more than one treatment or additional steps besides those listed here, and Resident shall cooperate in taking all listed steps and additional instructions from the licensed pest control professional as many times as needed to ensure the infestation is gone.

7. Resident agrees to pay landlord's losses or expenses for infestations that occur if it is determined more likely than not that the infestation is a result of Resident's occupancy or of any of Resident's guests. Anticipated losses or expenses include extermination fees, claims by other residents for their losses due to Resident's infestation, and attorney fees and court costs for evicting Resident for failing to comply with this addendum.

8. Landlord agrees to take the following steps once an infestation is suspected or discovered in Resident's unit or adjoining unit:

8.a. Landlord shall promptly inspect the unit once notified by Resident of suspected infestation, or if adjoining unit is determined to be infested;

8.b. Landlord shall promptly have a licensed pest control professional confirm whether there is an infestation, determine the scope of the infestation, and perform all necessary steps to eradicate the infestation at landlord's expense. The Resident may be liable for those costs under paragraph 7;

8.c. Landlord shall take all reasonable steps to prevent infestation from spreading to other units once it is discovered.

8.d. Landlord shall have information on hand to provide to Resident on how to spot bed bugs, how to protect furniture, how to prepare for treatment, and other matters related to preventing infestation and how to react when it occurs;

8.e. Landlord shall inspect for bed bugs during general, periodic inspections that occur as a part of the original lease agreement between landlord and Resident.

9. Landlord shall notify Resident if a nearby unit is found to be infected and Resident shall allow access to Resident's unit for inspection and comply with all steps set forth in paragraph 6 if the infestation is determined to also be in Resident's unit, regardless of whether the infestation started at Resident's unit.

10. Landlord shall not be responsible for any loss of personal property by Resident or guest(s) as a result of infestation. Resident agrees to carry personal property insurance to cover such losses.

11. Resident's default of this addendum or the lease shall entitle landlord to terminate Resident's right to possession of the unit. The following items are considered a material default:

11.a. Any misrepresentation by the Resident;

11.b. Resident's failure to promptly notify landlord of the presence of bed bugs;

11.c. Resident's failure to adequately prepare for treatment or cooperate with the licensed pest control professional (in the opinion of the licensed pest control professional);

11.d. Resident's refusal to allow the landlord to inspect the premises;

11.e. Resident's failure to have personal property insurance to cover personal property damages or losses;

11.f. Resident's action or inaction that prevents treatment of the unit or potentially exasperates or increases the bed bug issue.

12. By signing below, the Resident agrees the terms have been read and are understood.

Date: _____

Resident: _____

Resident: _____

Landlord: _____

~~~

Conclusion

These are just two examples of lease addendums we have seen more and more often in the past few years.

If you are interested in seeing the full list of forms for the state in which you own properties, please to visit Real Tenant History at www.realtenanthistory.com.

Made in the USA
Charleston, SC
15 May 2014